D1611147

Knight Rose Press
knightrosepress.com
Trumansburg, NY, USA

ISBN: 978-1-7339913-1-5 (hardcover), 978-1-7339913-0-8
(paperback), 978-1-7339913-2-2 (ebook)

Library of Congress Control Number: 2019908212

Chapter Illustrations & Cover Art
Cover art and layout by Scott Dawson.
Each chapter is also introduced by a continuous line
drawing by Scott Dawson. Each drawing was inspired by
the chapter's text, even if it's a *bit* of a reach
(see: Perfection)

Author's Note
I recreated events and conversations as faithfully as I could
from memory. I changed or omitted some names and
characteristics to maintain individual privacy.

For Amy, Elizabeth, and Xander

"*I see the distributed aspects of the Internet and technology playing a key role in the decentralization of the workplace. To be successful, I feel that one must have both a satisfying personal and professional life. Without a satisfying personal life, the professional will slip.*"
— **Scott Dawson, Fall 1997**

FOREWORD

I've worked remotely for twenty-one years. This book is about my experience working remotely as a full-time user experience (UX) designer and web developer. Twenty years is a lot of wireframes, web pages, and work-related travel. It is a variety of managers, projects, and remote cultures. Working remotely has been such a positive influence on my personal and professional life. I'm so excited to share the lessons I learned!

I worked (and work) for companies with offices in New York City. The Big Apple is the "mothership," if you will. I live five hours away in a small town outside Ithaca, New York. My wife and I built a custom home, live a fit lifestyle, and breathe country air. We have two wonderful children and one very happy rabbit. My business card says I'm a web designer and developer, but people who've worked with me are more likely to say I'm a really effective remote worker.

Remote work is on the rise in the United States. Gallup reported that, in 2016, 43% of U.S. employees worked remotely in some capacity, up from 39% in 2012. According to the 2017 State of Telecommuting in the U.S. Employee Workforce, the number of US workers doing at least half of their job from a non-office location more than doubled between 2005 and 2015.

When I tell people about my situation, they usually say they could never work remotely. They say it would take too much discipline. Then the questions borne from intrigue start:

- How do you stay motivated?

- How do you stay connected?

- How do you avoid staying "out of sight and out of mind?"

I've answered these questions (and many more) for friends and colleagues who want to work remotely. One of my colleagues asked me for tips in a poignant instant messaging thread. He was struggling as a new father who recently started working remotely. He was having trouble finding his groove and getting his work done. That messaging thread turned out to be the catalyst for this book.

If you've jumped into the weekly #RemoteChat devoted to remote work, we've already met each other virtually. I created the Twitter chat several years ago and moderate the questions each week. Read more about it at artofworkingremotely.com. It's a great way for remote workers to meet each other and share information.

This book contains my own (often humorous) stories from 20 years of remote work, tips for setting up a quality workspace, and behaviors and practices that contribute to success outside the walls of a traditional office setting.

In **The Making of Me**, I share stories that helped me grow professionally. The takeaways from each story will help you, too, wherever you work.

The Space covers the physical aspects of a quality remote workplace. How can you set up an effective work area? What infrastructure will you need? What about office pets? What should you wear? How can you keep from raiding the pantry?

The Habits reviews behaviors and practices that can contribute to remote worker success. How can you manage remote teams and be a good remote employee yourself? What is good communication and how can you promote transparency with what you're working on? What are the key habits employers are looking for in remote employees?

At the end of some chapters, you'll find tips and takeaways that I found valuable in each story.

If you're new to working remotely, I'm sure you will find something here that will help you get started on the right track. If you're a veteran, I hope you find a tip or two to help you have a renewed relationship with your remote work lifestyle.

I'd like to dedicate this book to my family. My wife has been with me on this remote work journey right from the start, supporting me through the tough times and celebrating the successes. My kids were born and raised during the years I worked remotely, and remote work's inherent flexibility helped me change countless diapers, be there for unmissable moments, and support them as they grew into fine young adults.

Here's to living the remote work life!

TABLE OF CONTENTS

I: The Making of Me

These are the stories that helped me grow professionally. The takeaways from each story will help you, too, wherever you work.

A Fresh Coat of Sirloin (1991-1995)

I worked at Taughannock Farms Inn, an upscale restaurant and B&B, during summer breaks in my college years. "The Farms", as locals called it, overlooked picturesque Cayuga Lake in Central New York. I started washing dishes there when I worked in high school. I graduated to bussing tables, helping in the kitchen, and waiting on tables as the years wore on. It was hard work and the hours flew by.

I also worked a second job in my alma mater's maintenance department. My shift was from 7:30 to 3:30, after which I took a short break at home to change, and resumed work at the Farms from 4:30 to closing time. The timing between the jobs was perfect. The schedule was grueling, but what an education! I arrived at the school's maintenance shed shortly after 7 and sat with the rest of the crew as they trickled in. Sometimes there were donuts on offer. I often drank the incredibly strong coffee. There was always playful joking and ribbing as the clock clicked closer to 7:30.

I worked on the painting crew. To call us a crew was generous: it was me and an adult named Melanie. I was an indoor cat, and the other summer intern was an outdoor cat: Brian (who was younger than me) got to mow lawn each day. I was rather jealous for a few reasons. He got to drive this huge tractor while I'd only experienced operating a small John Deere riding mower for my summer lawn mowing jobs. He got to be in the sun all day and would end his summer with bronzed skin. All I'd end up with was an office tan.

On our first day, Melanie asked if I'd ever painted before. "Never," I said. My parents had a house full of wallpaper. Melanie gave me a huge grin, saying "Well, you're gonna learn." She was patient and kind. She taught me everything about painting, both technique and mindset. To this day, I think of her every time I grab a brush and dip it into a can of paint. We painted classrooms, steel doors, bathroom stalls and outdoor railings. We used latex and oil-based paints. We cleaned paintbrushes to a pristine condition more times that I could ever count. We pondered whether walls needed two coats of paint … or not. I listened to (and gained an appreciation for) classic rock. Melanie wouldn't have anything else on the radio and in hindsight I wouldn't have it any other way. Whenever I have to do some work that requires a long stretch of focus, I reach for classic rock. Melanie taught me about teamwork, kindness, and a ton about painting. I'm so grateful to her for taking me under her wing.

I also learned many lessons at The Farms. If you've ever worked in the restaurant business, you probably learned a lot, too. I worked my way up through the kitchen jobs to what you'd call a prep chef, though the schedule simply said "kitchen." Dan was the chef. There were two of us helping, yet on some slower nights it'd be Chef Dan and me. My job had many facets:

- keep on top of the pots and pans (soaking is your friend)
- prep and cook the vegetables and potatoes
- prep the sides on plates as orders go out
- cook the vegetarian dish (usually a pasta dish)
- cook the seafood

I credit The Farms with my ability to prepare a perfect lobster tail.

The kitchen staff had their own culture and language. While far from comfortable, I was enough of a chameleon to fit in and be a full participant. We had a deep understanding of each other's roles and habits. You'd recall a well-oiled machine if you watched us during the peak of a busy evening. I still have habits from these non-choreographed dances. If I pass behind someone in a kitchen I reflexively say "behind you." Nobody bumps into anyone else in a professional kitchen, at least not after the first time. It was serious, hard work, but we knew how to have fun, too. I have a prominent nose (my mother says it is "distinguished") and my nickname came easy. They called me "Eagle Beak", or "Eagle" for short. Nathan, a few years my senior, took to calling me something more respectable. He called me "Awesome Dawson." I liked that.

I then spent a few lucrative years as a tuxedoed waiter. Most of the other waitstaff were women, but there were two other guys sporting bow ties with me. On busy nights we were all there, but some weeknights it was just the ladies and me. They were as curious about me, in my late teens and early twenties, as I was about them. They graciously included me in their conversations and asked me questions about myself. I interacted a lot less with the guys. They cared more about their appearance, the quality of their stud sets, and their tip income. They were into boats and drugs when they weren't hoisting trays. Unlike the kitchen, I couldn't figure out how to be a chameleon with them. My experience with boats was sailing in the Boy Scouts and Tylenol was my situational drug of choice.

I recall an evening with a problematic table of four guests. The experience was so out-of-band that I still remember where the table is in the restaurant. One of the guests was from out of the country and he was being entertained by his fellow patrons. We'll call him Tim for the sake of brevity. I could not make Tim happy. He complained to me about every part of his experience. For the main course, there was something wrong with each of the steaks that I brought him. Each time I brought a steak back to the kitchen, the chef cut into it. He was flabbergasted: each cut's doneness was exactly as ordered. I tried to get as much detail from Tim each time, but he became agitated. His dinner companions were soon finished with their meals. Tim's belligerence led me to do something I'd never done before. I composed myself. "Sir, I've tried many different ways to please you today, and I've concluded that this … is not possible." I regarded the others politely and set the bill on the table, absent a charge for Tim's meal. "I'm very sorry for the experience today, and I'll leave you now. You may relax as long as you'd like and pay your bill on the way out. Good evening." I left. I didn't check in on them again, and they didn't linger. As they walked out to their car, I went over to the table. Several corners of bills peeked out from under one of the plates across from Tim. The person who paid must have been mortified. I received the best tip I've ever received in the service industry. I'll never forget it.

Though I didn't relate to them much, I wanted to emulate the style of the two other male waiters. I started carrying trays above my head, up on my fingertips. Part of the job is performance: how you walk, how you smile at people, how you make them laugh. It's entertainment. As was tradition at the Farms, we memorized and offered to recite the lengthy dessert menu. Rattling off twenty or so delectable confections is impressive, especially if you make each one sound more delicious than the last.

I earned no style points one afternoon with a table of ten seated outside the swinging kitchen doors. They all ordered steaks and the meal was progressing well. Dan called my name when my order was ready. I stood across from him looking sharp in my tuxedo and coiffed hair. I had a large tray in front of me that could hold six dinner plates. I loaded it up and grabbed a smaller tray to hold the remaining four plates. I'd seen one of the other waiters do this before and I was sure it would work. One of the veteran waitresses eyed me with skepticism. She clicked her tongue and shook her head from side to side. Both trays were ready for flight. I picked up the big one and hoisted it over my head with my right hand. Five fingers bore the load of six perfectly-cooked steak dinners. My left hand was now free to pick up the smaller tray. I knew there were two tray stands set up right outside the dining room doors. I strode with authority toward the swinging doors. Another waitress chimed in almost under her breath, "Don't do it, Scott." I arrived at the door and used my foot to nudge it open. Problem was, it was a bit more than a nudge. The door ricocheted back at me as I was midway through the doorway. It smashed against the edge of the high tray, upsetting its balance. I let the smaller tray crash to the floor in a bid to rescue the larger lofted tray. Both trays ended up together at my feet. The shattering cacophony ceased all conversation in the dining room. Every pair of eyes turned towards me. I stood awkwardly in the doorway with one foot in the dining room and one in the kitchen. Large white shards of broken plates and $250 of perfectly-cooked beef littered the area around my feet.

I froze. I was in utter shock over what I had done. How could I deal with this mess? One of the proprietors, Nancy, was right around the corner and was at my side in a flash. To this day, I'm in awe of how calm and no-nonsense she was about the whole thing. I glanced through the kitchen doors and saw Dan nonchalantly yet begrudgingly throwing new steaks on the grill. This was not his first rodeo. With all of the dining room patrons' eyes on us, Nancy helped me clean up my disaster and cart the whole mess back into the kitchen. She didn't scold me, she didn't dock my pay, and she didn't hold a grudge. She knew I would be my own worst critic.

I never attempted that two-tray maneuver again. I did continue to put single trays up over my head as I flitted about the restaurant on other evenings. I'll forever be grateful for Nancy's deliberate, calming reaction to such a galactic mistake. When I encounter a crisis in adulthood I'm more likely to adopt that approach. I try to look at problems and crises through an analytical, dispassionate lens. It's a challenge, and not always successful, but it often has better results than the alternative.

Nancy and her husband Keith sold Taughannock Farms Inn to new owners Tom and Susan in 1997. I finished graduate school and moved to Long Island for my job. I enjoyed web design so I approached Tom and Susan with a business deal. I'd update and re-launch their website for free. It'd be the foundation of a freelance portfolio for me. I thought it'd be wonderful to get experience while helping an establishment I'd grown up in. They graciously accepted and compensated me with free meals. As the years went by we updated our agreement to include real money! I designed, developed, and upgraded their website for 19 years until new owners took over in 2016.

One last story of serendipity and prior relationships involves my wedding ring. My son played soccer and I was one of the coaches. It was a cold and rainy evening and few players had come to practice. I was kicking the ball around with the other coach and our sons. Daylight was fleeting and our sopping wet field was dimly lit by lights from a nearby football game. I took a shot on goal. With a flick of my thumb on my left hand realized in shock and horror that my wedding ring was no longer there! I immediately stopped and dropped to my hands and knees, horrified at the loss. The ground was a muddy soup. I searched by flashlight but realized the futility of the effort after an hour. Amy, my wife, knows that mistakes happen and she was quite cool about the whole thing. We resolved to have her ring melted down and be an ingredient for two new wedding bands. It was her idea.

I couldn't let it go that easily, though. I borrowed a friend's metal detector. I spent every minute I could spare methodically combing over a grid near the soccer goal. I found all kinds of interesting things over the span of a few days, but no ring. A few mornings later I was out on the field by myself in one last-ditch attempt before work started. Russ pulled up to the side of the field in a school maintenance truck. He had been a long-time member of the maintenance staff at the school. Russ was there many years prior when I was a painter with Melanie. I had enjoyed many mornings of witty banter with him. He grabbed the school's metal detector from the back of his truck and walked over with a wry grin. He said he wanted to help. He started working over near the center of the field, farther away from where I'd focused my search. His detector beeped and he reached down into the still-soft earth. He casually walked over to me, beaming. "Is this it?" I gave Russ the biggest hug I've ever given anyone! I reflected on his thoughtfulness in coming out to help me. I talked with Mike, his boss, as I brought an envelope back to school with a gift for Russ. I thanked Mike for allowing Russ to come out and help. Mike clarified that Russ hadn't really given him a choice. He said Russ matter-of-factly said he was going to go out and help me find what I was looking for. Relationships do help the world go around. It was heartwarming to see a relationship forged so long ago benevolently reach decades ahead and lend a hand.

Never use a second coat of paint when one will do.
Corollary: Never use a single coat of paint when the job clearly requires two.

Confronted with a stubborn baked-on, burned-on mess? It's far easier to soak a pot or pan instead of scrubbing for ages. Soak, then scrub. The analogy: when faced with a difficult problem, compartmentalize it and leave it for a bit. Go for a walk or a run, or work on something different. It'll still be there when you come back and the answer may come to you in the meantime.

There will be times when, despite your best efforts, you'll always come up short. Read the situation: know when to quit, and when to persist.

Keep a calm head in a crisis. Little good comes from being the one who panics.

Be nice to people and do not burn bridges. You never know where, when or how your paths will cross again.

PATHLIGHT (MAY 1995 TO JANUARY 1996)

I had a summer internship at Pathlight Technology in Ithaca, New York. It would be one of my first tastes of the "real world" before starting graduate school. I hung up my paint brush to make way for Pathlight. Waiting tables was still rather lucrative so I continued that as a second job to accrue as much cash as I could. Now that I was taking on student loan debt for a year of graduate school I'd need as much money as I could get!

I was assigned to work on benchmarking applications for storage area networks. I don't recall all the specifics of the software I wrote, but I do have other great memories from my summer at 9 Brown Road.

It was a stretch assignment for me. It went far beyond the confines of well-bounded academic assignments in Computer Science. I logged into Windows for Workgroups 3.11 and wrote code in Visual Basic or Visual C++ (I'm not sure which ... it was Visual something). I wrote applications to stress test the storage area network.

I felt both young and old in this job. I felt mature in the sense that I was working at a company in my chosen field with one more year of education ahead of me. I felt like a kid, though, since it was one of the first times I was "on my own". I realized that many of the decisions from here on out were mine. The buck stopped with me. It was a lot for me to process! I remember:

- I sped through Cayuga Heights one morning to get to work on time. I was so stressed about not being late that I drove 45 in a 30 in a neighborhood known for its police presence. When I got to the office, I called my Dad, crying. Yes, crying in my cubicle because I had gotten a ticket. Ah, youth.

- I ate lunch by myself most days. I chalk this up to me being an introvert, but I had an hour and I was going to use it. I never brought my own lunch, opting instead to drive to the mall food court and get Arby's or Wendy's. I sometimes drove to the lakeshore at Stewart Park to eat. Most days, though, I ate at a picnic table behind Pathlight's unremarkable building on Brown Road. What a missed opportunity! Not only was I eating fast food daily (people who know me now will laugh at this), I was spending all this time alone. I felt recharged most days and used the time for reflection, but it was like eating at my desk.

- I had to leave early several days a week to get to my second job at The Farms. I pulled out of the Pathlight parking lot at 4 and had to be 20 minutes away in a tuxedo at 4:30. I became rather adept at tying a bow tie using the rear view mirror! The schedule was a lot to manage and I found myself watching the clock as afternoons wore on. I'd love to go back and tell the younger me, "Think this is hard? Wait 'til you have kids, bro."

I was very task-focused during the early months of this internship. Once I was assigned something (and I'm still this way today), I had a strong, singular focus to get through it. That heads-down approach to project completion was not very satisfying. I felt a strong urge to "get through tasks" and see what lay waiting on the other side.

Later in the internship I started to come out of my shell and talk to other people. I walked by their desks, found out about their lives, and learned what they were working on. After a few of these encounters I no longer felt so isolated and disconnected. I could see how my work fit into a broader theme and direction. I appreciated what others were doing and saw how their work was connected to mine. These connections were the foundation of my support network. When I was blocked on a problem, I remember the relief of knowing who to turn to for help. In 1995, you couldn't simply Google the answer. Google sprung into existence in 1998. Quality content to feed search engines came after that. People are a fantastic resource! I began to appreciate that at Pathlight.

The most important experience I had lasted only five minutes. Said was Pathlight's cofounder and my boss. Pathlight was his first startup after working at IBM and he's since enjoyed a very successful career. I had to leave early to get to my other job and I was having trouble with a feature I was developing. I get upset when software doesn't work how it's designed to. Sensing my distress, Said stopped by and asked me what I was working on. I explained the problem and lamented that I had to leave shortly. I told him I'd have a chance to finish it up the following morning. I remember this vividly: he stood straight up with his brow furrowed. A knowing smile appeared on his face. He said, "I'm confused. How can you stop what you're doing in the middle of a problem? How will you sleep if you leave this development task unfinished?" He was projecting how he'd react if he was in a similar situation. The message wasn't lost on me. Logistically I couldn't stay and finish, but I wanted to. I felt the strong pull to get past the roadblock, to arrive at a milestone. Said had felt it enough times to be incredulous that I wouldn't stay and see it through. This became part of my work ethic over time: I have immense difficulty leaving tasks undone overnight. When I do, my brain works overtime to solve the problem. Sometimes it's not practical to stick it out to the end, though. Sometimes you have to take a break. It's a constant struggle! If I must leave something undone, it's so important that I compartmentalize it so I can disconnect.

Thank you for the lesson, Said.

There are few things in life worth getting a traffic citation for. Being late to a normal day at the office is not one of them.

If you work with a group, engage with them over lunch and breaks. There's always an opportunity to learn, share, and grow with others.

The people around you can help. They can also be helped by you. Talk to them: find out their interests, their hopes and their fears. Find out what they're doing. You never know how what you'll learn will help you in the future.

If you must leave something undone, try not let let it undo you. Compartmentalize your work. Be present for yourself and your family during your non-working time.

ARTIFICIAL INTELLIGENCE (1995)

My year of graduate work at Cornell was a whirlwind of courses and projects. I routinely worked with two of my classmates. We were inseparable! One of the memories that stuck with me, though, didn't involve them. I was taking an Artificial Intelligence class and they weren't in it. I don't remember if groups were self-selected or assigned but I ended up with someone I hadn't worked with before. We'd met once or twice but our circles didn't intersect due to our disparate course load. I was a graduate student and he was an undergraduate. Scheduling was difficult. We divided the project tasks up in our initial meeting. That was the last I heard from him.

As the weeks wore on I became concerned that our project would be incomplete. It was a significant part of our grade. My emails and calls to my partner went unanswered. In a bid to protect my grades I set up a time with the professor and spoke with her about my concerns. My partner was working on another important project and didn't appear to care about this one. The professor advised that I follow through on my commitments to the project. She suggested I document my efforts to communicate with my partner. She'd take that documentation into account along with my final project submission. I breathed a heavy sigh of relief and did exactly as she advised.

I received a good grade for the project and the class. I surmise that my partner did not. I never knew his reasons for bailing on me since we never had another chance to see each other outside of class. On reflection, though, I learned plenty from the encounter. Had I tried hard enough to work with him? I thought so at the time, but it would have been better to be more assertive. I could have sought him out and talked things through rather than relying on phone and email. Did a part of my subconscious prefer asynchronous communication? I am on the introverted part of the spectrum, after all. I also could have taken on most, if not all, of the work and learned something new along the way. Sure, I would have had to ensure the professor knew what I had done so I'd get proper credit. Since when has extra knowledge been a bad thing?

The subject of taking on more work and learning something new reminds me of the types of projects I took on early in my career. I specialized in building static websites for small businesses. When one business owner approached me with a requirement to include data from a database, I balked. I was so uncomfortable not knowing how to do anything beyond the basics! It wasn't the first project I passed on for that reason, either. If I had a partner who specialized in database work, I would have accepted the project. I didn't, so I just missed out on the opportunity. Years later, I'd have the chance to build more web sites with hefty database components, both at work and on the side. It wasn't so bad. I learned enough PHP and MySQL to build them, and the experience fed right back into other projects I was getting started with at work. Now, I know that I can learn pretty much anything, and the Internet can be a really good teacher.

I've also grown by putting myself in others' situations. Let's say I was my unresponsive partner. How would I have felt by leaving someone out in the cold like that? Not very good. I find that when I say I'm going to do something, I do it. A commitment is a promise. I might have to adjust and communicate but I never "go dark." This incident was formative in that way, too. There's plenty of group work in your future, whether it's on a team or working for a client or a manager. Inevitably, plans change because someone gets sick, has to tend to an emergency, or has a change in priorities. You have to expect those things will happen, and when they do, communication is more critical than ever. That's what helps people adjust their expectations, pick up the slack, or bring more resources into the fold.

As research into writing this chapter, I Googled my partner to see what I could find out about him. He made the rounds of some other prestigious institutions after graduating from Cornell. He's currently an associate professor at a university. He holds patents, published papers, and has a wife and son. He's an athlete and enjoys music. It's ironic: if we were neighbors in adulthood we'd be friends. Yet this singular shared encounter formed my poor impression of him.

You never get a second chance to make a first impression. Don't squander the opportunity to let someone see who you really are.

Do more than you've committed to do. You might learn something along the way!

Make sure you get credit for what you've done. If you're not clear about your contributions, people will have to guess.

If you commit to doing something, follow through.

25

THE INTERVIEW (1996)

I graduated from the State University of New York at Geneseo in 1995 with a degree in Computer Science. It was a wonderful four years. I discovered new areas of study, matured (as much as a college kid can), and met some great people. I met my future wife although we did not have our first date until several years later. I had the skills to start my career after getting my undergraduate degree. I wasn't inspired by the recruiters visiting Geneseo's career center, though. I didn't sign up for a single interview. I decided to go to graduate school.

Someone told me a graduate degree would give me more job options. I found out about Cornell University's Masters of Engineering in Computer Science. It was a compelling educational add-on — it'd take one year and a few extra summer credits. Plus, I was paying postgraduate tuition by myself, and one year of student loans sounded better than two. I applied early decision to the program. Cornell was close to my childhood home and I would be comfortable there (I was a bit of a homebody, too). After all, I had chosen my undergraduate school partly due to its proximity to my hometown.

I was elated as I read Cornell's acceptance letter in my small Geneseo dorm room. I had at least the next year of my life plan planned out now! I saved money from summer jobs and internships but I'd have to get a government student loan for the balance.

A year is not a long time. The first semester flew by and I was rapidly learning new things. You could find me in only a few places that year:

- a top-floor lab in Upson Hall
- attending a lecture
- eating waffles in Willard Straight Hall
- sleeping

As the calendar rolled from 1995 to 1996 I also frequented the career center in Carpenter Hall.

Cornell's career center was quite an operation. New companies arrived weekly, vying for the attention of Cornell's upcoming graduates. Microsoft. IBM. Motorola. Morgan Stanley. We were also vying for their attention! We pored over the sign-up sheets posted in Carpenter Hall. What companies seemed interesting to me? There was no real intention to this "job search." I hadn't thought about what I wanted so it was a scattergun approach to my professional destiny. I wasn't prepared for some of the more technical interviews. Microsoft didn't even call me back after my session with them. I signed up for as many interviews as I could. I knew that time spent interviewing was good practice.

I walked into the interview room at the appointed time for one of these "practice" interviews. A major bank had sent a representative to speak with job hopefuls like me. The interviewer started off with the softest of pitches over the plate. "So, Scott, what can you tell me about the private banking business?"

Shit.

I hadn't prepared for this interview. Heck, I hadn't prepared for any of these interviews. I assumed I'd talk about me, my skills, my path. Big mistake. How could I reply? As with most things in life, the truth seemed the best option and most in line with who I was.

"To be honest, I don't know what private banking is."

He smiled. The next half hour was surreal. My interviewer proceeded to have a discussion with me about private banking. A private bank provides financial services to the ultra-high net worth market. Ultra-high net worth meant, per the bank's definition at the time, $25 million in investable assets. In today's parlance: the 1%. It wasn't as straightforward as commercial banking technology. The business needed to support complex relationships, business structures, and products. The interviewer was so excited and enthusiastic as he told me about the business. The tables had turned: he was selling me on the position. Sure, it'd be attractive to work in Silicon Valley during the ascent of the technology boom. But a bank headquartered in New York City? Not so much.

I received a callback to go to New York for a full day of follow-up interviews. As luck would have it the interview fell on January 8, 1996, in the middle of the blizzard of 1996. The storm started two days before my interview and dumped over 20 inches of snow in Central Park. I flew from Ithaca to New York the evening of January 7. Manhattanites hunkered down during the city's fourth-largest single snowfall at the time. The cab's route from the airport to my hotel took me through deserted snowy Manhattan streets.

My upbringing prepared me well for what followed. I participated in group interviews but they were not the most memorable part of the day. We were asked to solve physical problems in small groups. The activity was likely designed to reveal leadership and collaborative tendencies. I tend to be an introvert but my youth scouting experiences helped me play the role of an extroverted leader. I led the activity, yet deferred to others when they had ideas and opinions. I sensed that we were being watched by managers roving the room. It must have been delightful for them instead of doing their "day jobs." I was enjoying it too! Lunch was also a thinly veiled part of the interview. We sat around expansive tables with formal place settings in the executive boardroom. I conversed with my fellow interviewees but didn't dominate the conversation. I cut my food into manageable bites. I used the proper utensils. I didn't chew with my mouth open and didn't talk with food in my mouth. In short, I tried not to show discomfort with what was not part of my daily culinary repertoire. I knew what they'd be looking for in this formal environment, given my experience at the Farms. Maybe it was just about the food for the bank, but I'm certain there was a component of judgement — active or passive. The entire experience pushed my social boundaries. I was out of my comfort zone. I could feel myself growing.

I had four career choices when my offers were in. I knew it wasn't a decision to take lightly: this was a fairly permanent choice! It would involve moving to a new city, making new friends, and having new hobbies. Each path could lead to a very different location years from now, too. I shared with my interviewers that my parents were "lifers" in their professions. I was looking for the same type of commitment from (and for) the company I'd work with. My mother taught in the same school district her entire career. My father worked at the same bank his entire career. I doubt this was something hiring companies were accustomed to hearing. This was during the ascent of a tech boom! Technology workers flitted from job to job, often in the span of a few years or fractions thereof. I was looking for a long-term commitment, not a job-oriented fling. I chalk that attitude up to my risk aversion. Not having to switch jobs — being a "lifer" — meant security. That sounded good to me.

- **Choice 1:** A big Wall Street bank in New York City.

- **Choice 2:** A military contractor in Vermont.

- **Choice 3:** A technology consulting firm in Virginia.

- **Choice 4:** Software development for the petroleum industry in California.

I chose New York City. I grew up in an upstate New York village with 2,000 residents. The country kid in me wanted to see the big city. *The Secret of My Success* is one of my favorite movies, in which Michael J. Fox makes a similar decision. I started with an 18-month rotation through business, regional and global technology positions. The variety of roles in this initial period helped give me a global mindset and position me for growth. I worked at the bank for 17 years (15 of them remote). I learned to work with varying management styles. I worked on different types of projects. I got the chance to work from home from a very foresightful manager. I have many stories from that first job and most helped me grow as a professional. It was an excellent decision.

There you have it: the story of one of the most important interviews of my life. The seeds of my remote work journey were planted during a practice interview. I didn't prepare. I told the truth, as embarrassing as it was. I didn't sense any of the anticipation or pressure of a life-changing event. I hadn't considered that I was sitting across the table from my future manager. Turns out I was.

Tell the truth. And oh, this theme will recur. I've never had a time when the truth didn't set me free.

CHUCKLES (1996-1998)

Reality hit after I accepted the bank's offer. I had so much to do to get ready! I'd be in New York City, far from home and without a ready-made support network. It wasn't college, with its built-in friends, dining halls, and few financial obligations. First order of business: I needed a place to live. Craigslist and other online apartment-finding sites didn't exist in 1996. I circled promising apartment listings in a newspaper before my first apartment-finding trip. Several weeks later, once in New York, I called one of the circled listing's numbers.

"Yes, hello? I'm interested in the apartment you've listed for rent."

The man on the other line was befuddled. In his thick Long Island accent, he asked, "What are you talking about, apartment? Where'd you read about this?"

I told him the name of the newspaper.

He was upset. "Bastards. Jeez." He muttered something else unintelligible. It wasn't the clearest phone line.

I cut in, "Would it be okay if I came and took a look today?"

"Sure," he replied begrudgingly. We agreed on a time.

We met at what I thought was a really nice apartment. It was on the second floor of a 2-story building in Mineola. The bedroom and bathroom windows looked out on the busy Jericho Turnpike. The kitchen windows looked west, let in plenty of light, and offered views of a parking lot and a firehouse.

31

Chuckles Comedy Club was downstairs. The landlord told me Eddie Murphy and Jerry Seinfeld had performed there. I could have tickets sometime if I took the apartment. I was sold! I told him I'd sign the lease.

"You're lucky, you know." he said. "This technically isn't on the market yet. It wasn't supposed to be in the paper until today. I called 'em, and it wasn't in yesterday's paper. I don't know how you read about it."

I offered him my newspaper with the circled listing, and we both realized at the same time what had happened. My newspaper, weeks old, advertised the apartment across the hall. It was no longer available and the apartment we were standing in was the new listing. The rental market was hot and none of these listings lasted long. This was serendipity. None of the apartments I circled would be available — I circled those listings ages ago with my red pen. I had hit a home run (apartment run?) on my first step up to the plate.

I don't remember going to a show at Chuckles, but my parents reminded me that we all did. Eddie Murphy and Jerry Seinfeld never stopped by. Regardless, I do have many memories from my two years of living above that comedy club on Jericho Turnpike ...

Truck 2: There was a very loud siren on the roof of the adjacent fire department. It blew whenever there was an emergency — morning, noon, and night. Both of my grandfathers were volunteer firefighters. I reasoned that I might as well get involved if I was going to be woken by the siren anyway. I joined the Mineola Fire Department's "Truck 2" company. We had two primary ladder trucks — 165 and 168. I learned so much from the drills and emergency calls on nights and weekends:

- cutting holes in roofs with a partner saw
- extricating people from cars
- putting ladders up and down
- climbing over parapets onto hot commercial roofs
- surviving training infernos at the Bethpage Fire Academy
- climbing the 110' aerial ladder and getting amazing views of Long Island
- rappelling off the side of a parking garage
- standing by for coastal nor'easters as they rolled in

I dressed up as Rudolph as we drove around in 165 at Christmas. I marched in full dress uniform in the Labor Day parade. I washed fire trucks, socialized with other volunteers, and solicited door-to-door for fund drives. I never got harassed in the early days for being a "probie" either. It was a true on-the-job education in the spirit of service.

Goodbye, Tonsils: I was chronically ill with sinus infections and sore throats. I visited ENT offices more often than a kid in his 20s should. One doctor told me my disfigured tonsils were destroyed by repeated inflammation. He suggested I have a tonsillectomy.

The procedure involved an overnight hospital stay and I was nervous. My parents traveled down to support me. When they stopped to visit me before I was discharged, they shared that they'd never had a worse night's sleep. I'd been sleeping on an old mattress with a depression in the middle and they kept rolling into each other. They'd gone out the next morning and bought me a new mattress. Sure, I lost tonsils in the deal, but I came out with a brand new mattress!

My girlfriend Amy came to visit for the weekend after my parents left. All she wanted to do was kiss me but I was in such pain that it was impractical. I was rarely sick after that surgery but I credit it only partly for a resurgence of my health. I'd soon be working in a home office from another state, no longer enduring the stress of a commute. It would have a profound impact on my health and well-being.

Cleanliness: I rarely cleaned my apartment. The bathroom was especially horrifying. I somehow didn't know what to do when pink mildew showed up in the shower! I let my clothes pile up so high it took 3-4 loads to get through them all at the nearby laundromat. Oh, how I longed for an apartment with a washer and dryer!

Nutrition: My bachelor eating habits are unrecognizable to me today. I didn't buy fresh vegetables or fruits from the local King Kullen, no. I microwaved vegetables with sauce in pre-wrapped plastic containers. I stocked my cabinets with boxes of pasta and Stove Top stuffing. I baked chicken with Shake 'n Bake but had to call my parents to find out how to thaw the chicken. I bought flats of Snickers at Costco and stored them in the freezer for an everyday treat. They never lasted very long, despite being out of sight. My movie snack of choice was a platter of cream cheese topped with cocktail sauce and popcorn shrimp. I'd eat most of it with several sleeves of Town House crackers. It is not coincidental that I weighed 15 pounds more than I do today.

Baratas: That's the Portuguese word for cockroaches. Mineola has a high Portuguese population and the roaches in the apartment moved in long before I did. They were not running rampant but there were enough of them to be a memorable part of my stay. They loved the kitchen sink and scurried across the kitchen floor at times. Amy visited during a school break and stayed alone in my apartment for the day. She sent me a frantic page (yes, I had a pager back before smartphones) and I called her as soon as I could. She told me she "trapped" a roach she caught scurrying across the floor. She grabbed one of my shoes and smacked it down on the unsuspecting critter. When I arrived home later that evening I picked up the shoe from the middle of the floor. The roach was gone. Not squashed or disintegrated. Vanished. The little bugger scurried off before impact, or weathered the blow and skulked out later. We had quite a laugh imagining the roach's inner dialogue! We're lucky we haven't had pests in any of our homes since.

Bright Lights, Not-So-Big City: The comedy club's marquee lit Jericho Turnpike's sidewalk beneath my bedroom windows. My dark green curtains and cheap faded blinds were no match for the glitzy marquee lights. They danced across my ceiling nightly. I could fall asleep during the week without a problem, but weekends were another story. As the club let out, laughing patrons lingered on the sidewalk and talked for what seemed like hours. I rarely dealt with that, though, after I started socializing more on the weekends.

I liked to go drinking and dancing with college friends from Smithtown and Central Islip. I returned home at 2 or 3 in the morning, or even later if we capped off our reverie with breakfast at a diner. Now, in adulthood, I'm in bed by 9:30 or 10! The fire siren wailed most nights, too. I'd get from a dead sleep to 100% prepared in the fire truck — bunker gear and all — within two minutes. Living next to the firehouse definitely helped my response time.

Domestication: I felt the pull to be a bit more domestic in that Mineola apartment. I decided I wanted to have homemade chocolate chip cookies one weekend morning. The immediate issue was that I had no tools to make them. I bought ingredients from King Kullen and a stand mixer and measuring cups from Roosevelt Field's Macy's. I unpacked it all in my apartment and made those cookies. Amy was smitten when I told her. I wanted cookies, so I made it happen! I also longed for my own Christmas tree. I have happy childhood memories of sitting in my parents' living room in the winter. I did homework with the room's semi-darkness cut by the tree's bright lights. I wanted to recapture that comfortable, cozy feeling so I went out and spared no expense on a 7' artificial tree. We still use it 20 years later.

Sick Day: I drove my car 7/10 of a mile to and from Mineola's train station as part of my commute. As someone who loves fitness in adulthood, I'm surprised that I didn't walk instead. I was definitely a fair-weather fitness person, but now I'll run with glee in the rain.

I remember feeling particularly lousy one morning. I endured breakfast and hopped in the car for the quick drive to the train station. As I passed side streets named after presidents I felt waves of nausea wash over me. I turned out on Washington and crept past by Jefferson and Jackson. I knew I was in trouble as I approached Lincoln. There was no inconspicuous place to stop the car. I wasn't about to get sick in someone's front yard!

I turned right and accelerated down Grant. Another right turn brought me back to the safety of my apartment. I parked my car out front so I'd have easy access to my door. I took the stairs two-by-two and slid my key into the lock. Another massive wave of nausea hit me as I flung open the door. I wasn't going to make it to the bathroom. The kitchen sink would have to do. It'd be a bonus if I nailed a roach with my repurposed breakfast!

After redecorating my sink I stood in the middle of my kitchen and took stock of the situation. I still felt horrible. My front door was ajar with my car out next to the curb. I decided I'd have my first sick day. I moved my haphazardly-parked car back to the parking lot, changed out of my suit and tie, and got back into bed.

Small Claims: I paid a hefty security deposit on the Mineola apartment. I was looking forward to receiving two months of rent when I moved out in 1998. I always paid on time, kept my apartment clean(ish) and never had complaints from the neighbors. I was shocked when the building's owner couldn't return the security deposit because "they didn't have it."

I ended up taking the building's owner to small claims court. The judge told me my claim was not against the building's owner. She said I needed to sue the landlord. The building's owner told the judge that the landlord fled the state and couldn't be found. The owner had been trying to recoup many months of past rent from tenants and the comedy club. We were both victims! I forfeited my deposit and developed a healthy attitude about it. I considered it a finder's fee for my first apartment. I lucked into renting it, after all, and had so many wonderful experiences there.

LATE NIGHTS AND EARLY MORNINGS (1996)

My boss was not in the office during my first day on the job. I got my security badge and made my way upstairs to the 18th floor. My teammates welcomed me and showed me my cubicle. The floor-to-ceiling window revealed an east-facing view of Long Island City. Long Island stretched off into the distance. It was beautiful. I asked the team a head-scratching question: "So, what should I work on today?" Clearly they had ideas of what they needed to work on, but they hadn't been briefed on what I'd do. One of them helpfully handed me a thick binder titled "Standard Interface Layer".

"You can start by reading this," he offered. "We built it!"

The languages I learned in school were going to be little use to me here. This was bespoke in-house software to help systems talk to each other. This was not my idea of fun but it was clear that I'd be expected to work on it in some fashion. I started to read.

I made steady progress as the week wore on. One morning just after 8 a.m. a group of my teammates were standing right outside my cubicle. They were talking about working late the prior the night on a production problem. I stopped reading and walked out to be in the periphery of their conversation. It was rather early in the day so my curiosity was piqued.

"Wait." I said. "You were working into the early hours of the morning, right?"

Sam nodded. "Yep."

"Then what are you doing here right now?"

My young brain was trying to process the logic. If you had put in extra time and effort and not slept much, couldn't you come in late? I naively said as much to Sam.

Sam grinned and scoffed at the notion.

"We have a job to do, and, well, sometimes that job requires a little extra effort. If we didn't come in today on time, there'd be other things that wouldn't get done. So we're here."

I admired the team for being so committed. They were responsible. Dedicated.

Sometimes I find myself in Sam's shoes. I get woken in the middle of the night to resolve production problems if I'm "on" for support. The call comes at midnight, or worse, 4 a.m. when it's almost impossible to get back to sleep. My team has had several weekends where a release went badly and we spent hours diagnosing the problem. Or, I've gone to bed really late after traveling and woke up on time, yet incredibly tired. When these things happen, I don't even consider missing meetings or showing up late. I know people are counting on my participation. I thank Sam and my original team for that work ethic.

Commit to your team. Extra effort will be required at times. Sometimes you'll have "down time" to work on other things. When you're expected to be somewhere, be there.

THE BRIEFCASE (1996)

My parents were proud of me and my big New York City job. They bought me a boxy briefcase with combination locks. As I commuted on the train, I noticed I was rather alone in carrying this kind of accessory. Most commuters carried laptop backpacks, soft-sided briefcases or commuter bags. I felt like I was carrying around state secrets and should have had the briefcase handcuffed to my wrist! My concern would be short-lived.

I left my office for the day and walked to the Long Island Railroad station at Hunterspoint Avenue. I passed the Mister Softee ice cream truck at the entrance to the station. I'll forever associate its signature jingle with this time in my life. I showed the conductor my train pass and secured it back in my briefcase. It felt so good to settle into the cushy seat after a long day of work. I nodded off before the train departed. I had ridden the route enough and felt comfortable that I wouldn't miss my stop. The train would pass through Jamaica just before my stop at Mineola.

The conductor began a spiel that I'd already memorized due to daily exposure. "This is the 6:08 train to Port Jefferson, making stops at …" (and dear reader, you must use a Long Island accent when dramatically reading this list)

Jamaica.

Mineola.

Hicksville.

Syosset.

Cold Spring Harbor.

Huntington.

Greenlawn.

Northport.

Kings Park.

Smithtown.

St. James.

Stony Brook … and …

Port Jefferson.

We'd arrive at Mineola after a half hour of gentle rocking as the train sped eastward. Some destinations farther along the track were from my past and some would be from my future. None mattered to me now, and I fell asleep.

I awoke with a start as the conductor announced "Next stop, Hicksville."

OH. MY. GOD.

I watched in horror as Mineola's train stop passed by my window. I missed my stop! I collected myself and took a deep breath. All was not lost. My train pass, phone and wallet were in my briefcase. I could get off the train in Hicksville and catch a westbound train to Mineola. I could also phone ahead for a cab to take me back to Mineola. I thought that'd be more expedient, actually. I fiddled with the combination lock on my briefcase to get to my phone. Remember, this was 1996 and phones were not designed to fit in pants pockets.

"That's odd," I thought. I must have messed up the combination.

I twirled the tumblers again on my fancy briefcase. No joy. I started to panic. I knew I was using the correct combination! I regretted having such a complicated briefcase when something simpler would have done. I did the only thing the engineer in me knew I could do on a moving train. I started at the beginning.

001. Click. 002. Click. 003. Click. 004 ...

I was panicking. The only resources I had to get turned around were stuck in a briefcase with a faulty combination lock. It was like some fictional yet plausible nightmarish game show titled "American Commuter."

061. Click. 062. Click. ... "This is Hicksville, Hicksville," the conductor's voice crackled overhead. 063. Click. 064. Click ...

"Next stop, Syosset." I sat up ramrod straight and remembered, "Hey, I know someone in Syosset."

I stopped my fumbling, tumbling and clicking. Adam and I were Resident Advisors at Geneseo together. I was sure he grew up in Syosset. I gathered my briefcase and coat and disembarked onto the sunny platform. The train pulled away and the rush of commuters passed by me. I politely asked one of them for a dime. With my brick-like phone locked in my briefcase, I needed to use a pay phone. Luckily, the phone book was intact under the platform's public phone. I looked up Adam's surname. Yes! There it was. I dialed and closed my eyes, hoping for the best.

I asked the man who answered the phone if he was Adam's Dad. Indeed, he was! He listened to my predicament and arrived at the train station a short time later. I was so grateful! He offered me a ride back to Mineola, but only after dinner at his house. He wanted to help try to free the contents of my briefcase, too.

That's how I found myself in a former classmate's house for dinner, just weeks into my new big-city job. I was grateful for the events leading to this impromptu reunion with Adam. I longed for social connection as I acclimated to the new apartment, new city and new job. Adam's Dad triumphantly returned from the basement.

"I had to break the lock. I hope it wasn't sentimental?" he said apologetically.

I thanked him profusely and told him it wasn't sentimental. I was so grateful he was able to open it! I knew my parents' hearts were in the right place but the broken lock was a silver lining. The fancy briefcase wouldn't go with me on any other train rides. A no-nonsense commuter backpack was in my immediate future.

Experiences can be quite different in hindsight. A hardship might result in a serendipitous reunion, or at least an excuse to get a new backpack.

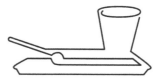

THE IMPORTANCE OF LUNCH (1996-1997)

I never ate lunch at my desk during my first 9 months in the Long Island City office. You're not alone if this surprises you. When I travel now, I see people eating at their desks while looking at a screen for news, entertainment or gossip. I've also seen people wolfing down lunch while on a mid-afternoon conference call. They let themselves get so hungry before succumbing to convenience food.

Howard, one of my teammates, walked down the corridor around noon on my first day in the office.

He sounded hopeful as he asked someone nearby, "Lunch?"

He was getting closer. "Lunch?"

He approached my cubicle. He playfully knocked on my cubicle wall's plastic housing.

"Join us for lunch?"

"Sure!" I said. We ate downstairs in the company's cafeteria. There were five or six of us that day. That would continue to be our daily routine until I left the group 9 months later to continue my rotation. Lunch was less about the food and more about the fellowship. We rarely talked about business. We talked about our lives. We sometimes sat with or near other close-knit groups, too. It was a great way to interact with people I wouldn't normally see during the normal course of business.

I remember so much from these team lunches. Howard was reserved and had a penchant for seeing the big picture. He carefully considered things before saying something profound and intelligent. Walter shared about how driving a cab taught him how to relate to people from all walks of life. FY was quiet and listened carefully to conversations as he ate. I learned that he was very much a family man and loved his social connections.

I visited that building sometimes when I worked with different teams later in my career. I lament that I never recaptured the small-team dynamic I loved during those first months. I visited the cafeteria during one of the trips. I grabbed my lunch by myself and walked by empty tables on my way back upstairs. I recalled how much value I got out of eating with my colleagues. It was surreal to be in such a memorable place, but to not see others make those same memories. Nobody sat talking in large groups and the echoes of our conversations had long since faded. I'll never forget Howard's light knock and invitation to lunch. The memory will always make me smile.

I take most of an hour for lunch now. I put a daily appointment in my calendar to prevent conflicting meetings. If it's nice outside my wife and I go for a 20-minute walk around the neighborhood after eating on our deck. If the weather's bad, we read books or watch the rain fall outside as we catch up under the shelter of our back porch. When I'm home alone, I watch an episode of a show, play my guitar or go for a short walk by myself. Regardless, lunch is an oasis in the middle of the day, and I take the time to revel in it!

Give your brain a break and take time for lunch. You'll be fresher when you return, ready to tackle the afternoon's challenges. Make an appointment with yourself in your calendar.

Be social with your colleagues outside of your daily responsibilities. It'll help strengthen and enrich those relationships. You'll be a better person and colleague by knowing who they are. What do they like? What are their fears? You'll realize that they, like you, are human. Keep your ears open and listen. You'll learn a lot. There's a reason I remember the names and faces of my colleagues from my first job, even 20 years later.

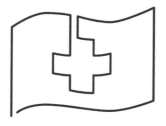

ASK AND YOU MAY RECEIVE (1997)

I wasn't interested in programming middleware, but that's what they had me working on. I was enamored with the Internet, especially front-end design and usability. Brochureware was a popular term at the time. It described web sites that were simple and static, like a brochure. Our corporate public website was brochureware.

Our internal web site — our intranet — also needed help. There were a handful of useful pages and they were hard to find.

Wayne Gretzky famously said "You miss 100% of the shots you don't take." With this in mind, I approached my manager with suggestions for improving our web sites. I offered to help, too. I wanted to work on internet or intranet projects.

It was a turning point in my career. As a result of the meeting, I'd pack my bags to work in our Swiss office that managed the company's European intranet. These types of projects would stretch off into the horizon, all a result of that conversation:

- Europe intranet
- Global intranet
- Client-only web site
- Certified Usability Analyst certification

- Internal application design
- New public web site (twice!)
- Prototyping
- Usability reviews
- Information architecture and content management
- iOS design

The list goes on. I worked on all aspects of website design and development during my tenure at that first job. I facilitated this priceless on-the-job experience by advocating for myself. I'm still very goal-driven and dialed into my likes and dislikes. I'm pragmatically vocal about what I'd like to see changed in my professional world. I say pragmatic, since some things are downright futile in a corporate environment. When futility is not a factor, though, speak up. Sometimes the answer will be no, as hinted by the title of this chapter (you may receive). Sometimes, though, asking can make all the difference.

If you want something, put together a plan to get it. If you don't plan, you can't act. If you don't act, you can't achieve.

Zum Mitnehmen, Bitte (1997)

I worked in Zürich from April to June in 1997. It was the second part of my technology rotation. I had not yet ventured far from my home state of New York. Working internationally reinforced how vast the world is. Europe felt so different, yet very much the same. I saw people going to and from work, dining out, traveling and socializing. Geography, culture, and circumstances are the things that separate us.

My journey started with a week-long trip to find an apartment and have a brief orientation at the office. I flew into Zürich's Kloten Airport a month before my rotation started. I cleared customs and took a short train ride into Zürich. It took me a while to find my hotel. It was dark and starting to rain outside. I checked in and raced to my room. I closed the door, dropped my bags to the floor, and started crying. I didn't even turn on the lights. I felt such despair. I felt like an imposter. I didn't have a shred of world experience. I felt like I'd "pretended" my way through international travel and customs. I was about to spend a week in a foreign office with total strangers. The pity party continued for a few minutes. The tears stopped rolling as quick as they'd started. I rolled my shoulders back, heaved a final sigh and said, "You can do this."

I returned to Zürich a few weeks later and moved into a small studio apartment. The walk to the office was short and delightful. I spent workdays improving an Oracle-based regional intranet. I immersed myself in culture and traveled on the weekends. My Eurail Pass whisked me away to wonderful destinations.

I went to the Flower Clock (L'horloge fleurie) and the Patek Philippe Museum in Geneva. I never made it past the front door at this watch museum. Instead, I spent the whole time talking to the security guard using my broken high-school French. It was a testament to my loneliness that I would talk to anyone who would talk to me! He told me he was thrilled to speak with someone who was making such an effort.

I was saddened by the bears confined in the 19th century Bärengraben Bear Pit in Bern. They were such beautiful, powerful animals. I toured the Bundeshaus, the seat of Swiss government. I learned that the CH on those white oval car stickers meant "Confoederatio Helvetica."

I journeyed to northern Switzerland to see Europe's largest plains waterfall. The Rheinfall illustrates nature's awesome power. I was there on a sunny day and it was spectacular.

I took a short boat ride on Lake Zurich to Rapperswil. I stood on cobblestone streets and saw the end of a fairytale wedding. A newly-married couple was pulling away from a castle in a horse drawn carriage. It looked like a movie set! There were no movie cameras and no director, though: it was real life.

I biked 30 miles round-trip to where one of my colleagues lived in Baden. The ride would have been uneventful had it not been raining. Before leaving Zürich's city limits, I almost hit a pedestrian as my wet brakes stunted my stopping power. It was one of the few times I was called a "stupid American" in the local language.

Amy and I spent a weekend in central Switzerland's Engelberg during her first visit. It sits at the base of Titlis in the Uri Alps mountain range and hosts a great ski resort. I didn't know how to ski at the time so we shared a monstrous gondola with a crowd of German-speaking skiers. We walked through the glacier cave at the summit. We attended an Easter service (in Swiss-German) at the charming Holzkapelle church. We understood little but it was quite enjoyable and appropriate to the occasion.

Lugano is the most beautiful city I've ever seen. I stayed in a hotel with postcard views.

I ventured into Italy and visited Milan (which I felt looked very much like Queens), Florence (who could miss seeing David), and Pisa (yes, I got a picture of me "holding up" the leaning tower).

Lugano was the most memorable place I visited. It was stunning and beautiful, yes, but I also had a life-changing realization there. I had finished eating dinner alone at a fantastic restaurant. I looked across the lake at amazing views of Monte San Giorgio and Italy beyond. I realized at that moment that I didn't want to be alone anymore. Amy planned to visit again near the end of my 3-month stay. I started making plans to propose marriage.

I told my colleagues and they were so excited to help in any way they could! My first challenge was the ring. Amy shared with me that she didn't want a ring if she ever got engaged again. She was engaged once before and had called it off. What could I get instead of a ring? One of the guys in the office suggested I go to Tiffany on Bahnhofstrasse. Why didn't I think of that? I walked into their centrally-located storefront and explained my predicament. The salesperson offered many options and I selected a silver perfume flask in the shape of a heart. I had them engrave it with "I give you my heart" and, in a bold show of confidence, the date I planned on popping the question! There'd be no margin for error.

Amy grew up all over the world in a military family. She lived in Germany for a few years, so we planned to go to Garmisch and Berchtesgaden after some time in Paris. I planned a Parisian proposal. I must have had a goofy grin on my face during the train ride to Paris as Amy kept eyeing me with suspicion. More than once she asked "What's going on?" Each time I said I was just so happy to see her! We were so hungry as the train pulled into Paris mid-afternoon. We ordered a plate of mozzarella cheese, tomatoes, and balsamic vinegar from a nearby restaurant. I wasn't a fan of tomatoes but in my smitten state I didn't care. I love that dish now — what a wonderful way to embrace tomatoes!

It was time to find our hotel, but via a meandering route. I knew I had to propose on the way since today's date was engraved on the flask. We went up the Eiffel tower and looked out over the beautiful cityscape. We crossed the Seine on the Pont d'Iéna and walked along the grounds of the Palais de Chaillot. We were getting closer to our hotel and I knew I'd need to ask soon. It was now or never. I stopped and asked her to sit on a low wall along the green expanse. The ground was wet from recent rain and kneeling would get my pants dirty. I awkwardly squatted and popped the question. I was so nervous! It came out as less of a question and more of a statement of desire. I opened the Tiffany clamshell containing the perfume flask.

"I want you to be my wife!"

She said yes! We were so happy as we continued our walk. A few minutes later she told me how much she loved the flask. Then she tactfully said that despite telling me she didn't want a ring, she'd want one after all. We shared a wonderful laugh and I promised to buy a ring with her when we were back in the United States.

Our printed map was not very detailed and we were lost after a few more minutes of walking. Things are far different now with the availability of phone-based maps! I asked another pedestrian if he could help us find our way. In the course of conversation, this Parisian discovered that we were a newly-engaged couple. He was so taken by this that he offered to escort us to our hotel. He said it was on his way home anyway and he was happy to spend time with us! It's amazing what you can communicate using broken high school French. We walked for a few minutes as a trio. I began to sense that we were going in the wrong direction since the hotel wasn't far from the Eiffel Tower. I asked him to stop for a moment and clarified the directions with him. His face furrowed as he scrutinized the address. He slapped his palm to his forehead. He was walking us to Rue de Longchamp. Our hotel was the opposite direction on the smaller Rue du Bouquet de Longchamp. He said he was so sorry and embarrassed and started walking us back the direction we'd come from. I told him it was not necessary now that we had our bearings but he insisted. I will never forget this man's generosity! He went so far out of his way to help us. As soon as we were checked into our hotel we called our parents to share the news.

We vacationed in Garmisch and Berchtesgaden. The rivers in Garmisch flowed with a blend of vibrant blues and greens. We enjoyed a slow, bacon-heavy breakfast in Berchtesgaden and hiked to the top of the Jenner on the Königsee. I bought tickets for Celine Dion's concert at Zürich's Hallenstadion. We enjoyed a modest dinner of röschti with Heineken in my small apartment after the concert. It was a fantastic week.

My experiences in Switzerland are so vivid and rich. I've never had so many montages all stacked up against each other in my mind's timeline. Here are a few more memories that never fail to make me smile.

Sechseläuten: Most of my walks along Zürich's waterfront were quiet and contemplative. One weekend walk was quite the opposite as I encountered the end of a parade. The marchers gathered around a pyre, at least 15 feet tall, topped with a snowman effigy. The festival of Sechseläuten climaxes with the burning of the combustible pile. The effigy on top, known as the Böögg, represents winter. The faster the Böögg's head explodes, the more likely a warm, sunny summer. It was amazing to hear the cheers of the crowd as the flames grew and the Böögg lost his head.

Lunching at Steinway: I love music. I didn't have venues to play my trumpet after graduating from high school, but I did start playing piano in college. Oh, I learned the beginning bars of so many songs! My parents bought me a Korg keyboard after college graduation. I left that home (it's so heavy!) but I found a Steinway Piano Gallery on Limmatquai. I went there during many lunch hours to play on the pianos and walk around the glossy showroom. I was alone in the shop the first time I went and I noticed several store employees watching me. I stopped playing and apologized if I was being disruptive. They told me it wasn't a problem, that they loved hearing me play! I kept coming back and played whenever I could. It was such a restorative and joyful way to spend a few minutes in the middle of the work day.

Alice? Who's That? I worked in my company's office on Reitergasse. Like a Swiss watch, someone wheeled a cart into our space twice daily saying "Grüezi mitenand, it's coffee time!" I loved this Swiss-German/English greeting of hello and the promise of caffeine. Most people stopped working and headed over for their favorite pastry or beverage. The office culture was unlike any other I've worked in since: it was a healthy balance of fun and work. Take music, for example. Headphones (isolation booths?) were not that popular in offices yet. We turned on the office radio in the afternoon. I remember when a song's chorus surprised me enough to stop working and start looking around the room. Profanity, and lots of it! My colleagues realized this was something new for an American. There's no FCC in Switzerland, after all! Smokie's catchy refrain of *"Who the Fuck is Alice"* reverberated through the office. Everyone sang along like we were mates in a bar. I bought the CD that afternoon.

Working 9-5: Nobody burned the midnight oil. The Swiss in my office prided themselves on work/life balance. They arrived and left with punctuality. What is the point of work, one colleague said, if you can't enjoy life? One evening I was working late on a project I'd given an aggressive deadline. I packed my things at about 9 p.m. and started to leave. The building's lights were off and the exterior doors were locked from the inside! Panic set in. I paced throughout the building looking and yelling for anyone. I called my boss at home from an office phone. I could almost hear him grinning on his end of the line. He asked why I'd been working so late and advised I let someone know next time. He then told me how I could call the security office for some help leaving the building.

Sorry, but we speak English here: I arrived in Switzerland hoping to learn the local language. I would be disappointed, though. Most people I interacted with — in shops, in the office, or at restaurants — spoke perfect English. The only place I found where English wasn't spoken at all was a dry cleaner. I pantomimed to communicate with them. My "cultural immersion" hadn't forced me to pick up the language. Of the choice Swiss-German phrases I picked up during my stay, my favorite is this chapter's title. *Zum mitnehmen, bitte.* I used it when I ordered lunch from a deli near the office. I pointed at the items I wanted and read the tight Swiss-German script on the card in front of them. I knew the next question asked of me, in Swiss-German, would be "Would you like that to stay or to go?" Zum mitnehmen, bitte. I'd like that to go, please.

Rollerblading without Words: I joined Luxor Fitness on Glärnischstrasse. I loved to play racquetball and Luxor had squash courts. Cousins, at least! I played a few squash matches with friends from work and one interaction had them in stitches. We were cleaning up in the locker room and they saw me using shampoo from back home. They were especially intrigued by the label: it advertised how good it was for "limp" hair. Of course they took this as a sexual reference and joked about me using shampoo to combat limpness. Juveniles.

This wasn't the only word that didn't translate well. "Diet Coke" for example, was "Coke Light" in Switzerland. I was curious enough to ask my office mates about that. They said if you preceded any product with "Diet" it'd be interpreted as being for fat people. Shrewd marketing move, Europe.

Anyway, back to the gym. I checked in one day holding the roller blades I used to get there. The front desk person gestured to them and asked if I would lead a weekend rollerblading group. I was flattered and accepted the offer. I found a group of eager rollerbladers at the gym at the agreed time. Keep in mind, I'm an expat American who didn't speak much Swiss-German. Not a single person in the group spoke English! You know what, though? We had a fantastic time. All I had to do was skate and do my best to communicate with the group. We happily skated a meandering route along the waterfront for the better part of an hour.

It's the Tonight Show: I missed home but the alternating busyness of work and travel made time pass quickly. Jay Leno helped with the homesickness, too. I didn't miss a single episode of The Sky Channel's nightly broadcast of his Tonight Show. Familiar food and English movies also helped stave off homesickness. One of my go-to evenings was dinner at Subway and a movie at KITAG Cinemas Capitol on Weinbergstrasse. I also enjoyed walking and exploring. My walk to Uetliberg stands out in my mind. I followed a dirt path next to a rolling field with a solitary tree standing in the middle of it. The color of the sky and spring temperatures made me feel tranquil and peaceful. I took a photograph but the picture in my mind is far more colorful. Whenever I'm stressed or need calm (blood draw, anyone?) I close my eyes and think of this scene.

Don't Die Yet: I was sick a lot when I lived by myself on Long Island. I felt healthier in Zürich, but still felt the occasional malaise. One weekend in Italy I awoke to night sweats so bad I thought I was dying. I shared my concerns with Amy.

Unbeknownst to me, she set about diagnosing me online. Her Internet search concluded that I had Non-Hodgkin's lymphoma. I had an odd underarm rash that amplified my alarm. I was in full panic mode and made an appointment with a Swiss doctor. I'm quite the hypochondriac. The time between having blood drawn and getting the results was interminable! I was beyond grateful, then, when the doctor shared the results. No cancer. Completely normal blood test. He chalked the night sweats up to a very bad cold.

To this day, I sweat at night when I'm feeling subpar or particularly stressed. The rash cleared up after he advised I use a different soap. Amy and I breathed a sigh of relief and shared a good laugh. When Amy tries to diagnose things online today (we're all dying, aren't we?) I remind her of Zürich, night sweats and a bad brand of soap.

Coming Home: My manager, Rene, invited me to his hometown for a weekend festival near the end of my trip. I think he sensed my loneliness. It was a testament to his character that he took such an interest in me. I remember him picking me up Saturday morning in his car since trains didn't have routes to his town. I reflected on my experience as he drove out of Zürich. A new country. New languages (kind of). New friends. A fiancée! It was almost time to go back to that gleaming emerald tower that rose like a phoenix from Queens. I was a different person, though. I felt so blessed as I walked through the sun-drenched avenues of the small rural Swiss town's festival. I spent a lot of time alone on the trip, but through my interactions with others I found out who I was. Independence had set me free.

THE SINGAPORE INQUISITION (1997)

The bank sent me on a week-long trip to Singapore. I would analyze requirements for a new foreign exchange trading system. I wasn't sure I was the best person to send, given my lack of knowledge about trading and foreign exchange. I thought I'd get by with my inquisitive nature and the book I bought to study on the plane.

The flight on Singapore Airlines was amazing. I sat in a comfortable business class seat that had ample storage beside my left leg. I had everything I needed at arm's length for the long flight. It was a welcome departure from cramped domestic US flights. Despite all this, I arrived Sunday at 6 a.m. feeling quite shabby. I asked my hotel's front desk for a teakettle and spent most of Sunday drinking tea and sleeping. The jet lag and malaise abated by mid-afternoon and I ventured outside. I went into a department store and headed straight to the housewares section. I enjoy looking at dishes and small appliances. I bought a 6-pack of sturdy Claytan ceramic bowls as a souvenir (I still use them 20 years later).

I had a lot to learn from the team in Singapore in five days. A very affable local employee escorted me from meeting to meeting. Most were uneventful, but one interaction was very memorable. I met with a senior manager and asked him a question about why an existing application was built the way it was. He offered an answer but it was vague and not helpful. I asked the question a different way. Same type of answer. Either he didn't know or he was being cagey. I tried yet another approach and my handler abruptly ended the meeting. He apologized to the gentleman we were meeting with.

I didn't think I'd been rude but I had been persistent. My Singapore colleague directed me to never question a superior. I was shocked! How can you have a rule like this? In preparation for the trip, I read about the things that could land you in jail or get you fined. I knew about chewing gum (don't import it), drugs (draconian punishments for use and trafficking), and tipping (it isn't customary). Was it a cultural custom to not question a superior in Singapore? I was asking a very targeted "why" question that would have helped me do my job. I still don't know if this is a custom or just a quirk of the specific local office culture at my company. I apologized but I didn't mean it. I didn't understand. I've never received another admonition like that despite my continued inquisitiveness.

The rest of the trip was uneventful. I enjoyed evenings poolside at the hotel reading my book about foreign exchange. I never had a hand in building that foreign exchange system but I learned a ton about foreign exchange. I can still tell you where you can spend a "bhat" and what countries refer to their currency as a "dollar." No matter what I learn, it usually comes in handy at some point down the road.

Whether encountering a new country, a new culture or a new person, know your audience. Do your research. Ask questions. It'll help tailor your interaction for success.

GO HOME, YOUNG MAN (1997)

My remote work journey was about to begin. The prior chapters chronicled the rotation program at my first job. I worked in technology groups in New York and Zürich and marketing in New York. Eighteen months later I started my "permanent placement" role in Long Island City. Amy and I were engaged now and planned a wedding the following summer. It was an exciting time in my life! I was surprised to find this prescient note I wrote to my senior managers in 1997. It was for a "Management Resource Inventory." They wanted to understand what I saw as my professional future. This paragraph was part of my "long-term goal" answer. Ironically, I wrote this before the idea of remote work came up with my manager the following year.

> *I'd like to explore further the concept of offsite work. I see the distributed aspects of the Internet and technology playing a key role in the decentralization of the workplace. To be successful, I feel that one must have both a satisfying personal and professional life. Without a satisfying personal life, the professional will slip. Therefore, my personal preferences of staying on the East Coast, eventually moving away from the metropolitan area as I*

start a family, are key in ensuring a fruitful professional life for me. — Management Resource Inventory, Fall 1997

I asked for some time with my manager on a sunny morning in 1998. He always listened, provided thoughtful responses, and showed creativity in his solutions. I wanted to settle my career direction before getting married. Amy and I explored myriad housing options in New York and on Long Island but nothing seemed to fit. I was restless and began see job change as an avenue to geographic change.

There are many adages about truth. Being honest about my feelings and preferences can yield good results. Being truthful to yourself is the first major step. I held a good job in New York City yet my heart was telling me that it wasn't my path. My company didn't have a remote work option. You may think me naive for doing so, but I told my manager the truth. I told him I was about to be married and wanted to live in another area. I wanted to let him know I was going to be searching for jobs — either an internal transfer or a job with another company. I had no other angle. No other motivation. He considered what I said. After a few moments he asked, "How would you like to work from home?"

I was really surprised. Sure, I had floated the concept of working remotely in the Management Resource Inventory, but it had never been done in my department. I never thought it would happen this quickly and it addressed my concerns. I could keep my job and live where I wanted to. Amy would be able to teach in Massachusetts.

"I could work anywhere, like in Massachusetts?" I asked.

"Sure," he replied. "You can work anywhere as long as you can get to New York without too much hassle."

Delta operated an hourly airport shuttle between Boston and New York. This was going to work out great! I was on top of the world, eager to usher in my new life as a remote worker.

We rented a 3-bedroom apartment in Waltham, Massachusetts. The bank paid to install a "high speed" ISDN connection — twice as fast as dialup! We realize in hindsight that a 2-bedroom apartment would have sufficed. Amy was away teaching all day so it was too much space for a couple with no kids. Otherwise, it was the perfect place to start working remotely.

Be honest with yourself. Only then can you take action to get what you truly desire.

Be cautiously candid in your communications. Sure, there are times to be cagey, but straight-up truth is usually wiser. *Corollary:* Look out for people who may take advantage of you. Politics thrive in workplaces. It's shrewd to know people's motivations before entering a negotiation.

WHAT'S THE FREQUENCY, KENNETH? (1998)

I started working remotely from Waltham. A short time later, I also started working for a new manager. After a brief period of working with her, she told me I wasn't meeting her expectations. My work was fine but she wanted me to see her more often. I had agreed to travel a few days each month with my prior manager. She had other plans.

"Scott, how can you come here for a few days each month? It's not enough."

I replied, "I have been doing this for awhile now and it seems to be working. Should each trip be a few days longer?"

She continued, "I'm going to need you here for a few days each week."

I felt as if I'd been sucker-punched. A few days each week? I asked her why, trying to keep my emotions in check.

"If we're going to have a relationship, you and me, that can't happen if you're only here once a month. What if I'm out of the office those few days? Then I'm going to have to wait a whole month to see you?"

I replied, "But you have people that report to you from London, and they don't travel here each week."

That was upsetting, and her tone became emphatic. "Scott, that's different. I said I wanted you here every week, and that's what I meant."

I'm grateful that she was like one of the "bungee bosses" of Dilbert fame. She was here, then she was gone. I don't recall exactly how long I worked for her but I did obey her request … to a degree. Conflicts arose and I ended up traveling with about half the frequency she desired. There is a fine line to trip frequency. Her desire for more "face time" was for her benefit, not mine. Travel should benefit both parties. Some of my managers didn't prioritize face time at all. One in particular let me go a stretch of nine months without a trip! That's a bit too long, but it sure made the group's travel budget look good.

I'm in charge of my own travel. I usually travel 2-3 days every quarter for meetings or project kickoffs. I make a point to meet people who joined the team since my last trip. Most travel has a social component. Teams work well when social connections are strong. It doesn't take much — just a few social interactions and working together in the same place for a few days.

I'm far more productive at home. That's the primary thing that keeps me from traveling too much. I hate the backlog of project work and emails that greet me after a trip. It's harder to keep on top of things in the office, since opportunities for distraction abound. Meetings, hallway conversations, and noise pollution all conspire to kill productivity!

Travel has its place, but there's no place like home for getting things done.

When you meet a new manager, talk about their expectations. Strive to meet them but don't be taken advantage of.

Safeguard your time. Don't be bullied into traveling more often than necessary.

PEOPLE MAKE THE PLACE (1998-2001)

It was what I now call "early days" — an exciting time for the Internet. My team was building a new website for clients. We called ourselves eServices. It wasn't popular (yet) to prefix names with "i". Apple would not release iTunes, and all things "i", until January 2001. I joined the team remotely and traveled to the New York office at 425 Park Avenue a few times a month.

I've worked with many teams over my career. I got lucky early. eServices had the most hard-working, genial, and respectful professionals. We were an untested team building a new, cutting edge product. The mission contributed to the close-knit nature of the group. We also had an effective management duo leading us. They split their focus between the marketing and technology aspects of the product. There wasn't much bureaucracy. We each brought different ingredients to the table and the dish turned out to be delicious. My eServices experience was one of the highlights of my career.

The company encouraged professional development. I attended IBM's "Make IT Easy" conference for several years. It was one of the earliest user-centered design conferences. It cemented my affinity for usability. I brought ideas back from the conference and applied them directly to the project. I took a series of courses and exams from Human Factors and became a Certified Usability Analyst.

Our iconic Park Avenue office building sat across the street from Swissotel The Drake. The hotel has since been rebuilt as private condominiums. Now it's the tallest residential building in the Western Hemisphere, but I'll always remember the Drake. The commute to the office was laughable by New York standards. I stepped out one building, crossed Park Avenue, and entered another building. I loved using the Drake's lavish fitness center. It was so clean and comfortable. We modeled our home gym partly on their fitness center.

I enjoyed a cheerful "Good morning, Mr. Dawson!" every time breakfast arrived in my room. The tray overflowed with coffee, orange juice, English muffins, and jellies from Fauchon. The centerpiece was a generous helping of traditional Swiss Bircher Muesli. Fauchon is a French gourmet food and delicatessen shop still in operation today. I regret not walking into their street-level storefront. I would have enjoyed at least browsing their wares! Amy loved it when I brought the extra jelly from my breakfast tray home!

Another note on the Fauchon reference: years later we worked on the company's brand. The brand agency likened our company to a Fauchon storefront. The warehouse behind it was akin to a Home Depot filled with products and services. Clients received high-touch personalized service backed by a veritable hardware store of products. The Fauchon reference needed to be explained to a lot of people, but I got it right away. It was all because of the jelly and the delightful Drake.

Our team went our separate ways after the website launch. I kept in touch with a few of them over the years. We shared wedding celebrations, sadness in the wake of losses, and more than one's fair share of grappa. The experience taught me that it's not what you're doing that makes something special, it's who you're doing it with. People make the place.

Look at the people around you, at work or at home. As Tim Ferriss says, "You are the average of the five people you most associate with." If you don't like those five people, you should make some changes until you do.

Shut Up and Eat Your Banana (2002)

I worked for some wonderful managers. I also experienced the pain of working for some awful managers. I learned a lot from the them, but those lessons are in the "never treat people this way ... ever" category.

One in particular was a tyrant. I resisted and came out winning in the end. My time on her team was uncomfortable, and while it is tempting to recount my experiences in detail in this chapter, it would only serve to make me feel better. So, I'll summarize what went down for your reading pleasure. We'll call her RBM (Really Bad Manager) for the sake of anonymity.

When RBM took over our development group she used policy as a weapon. Though I was not doing development work (I was a designer), I was labeled as a developer. I railed against several policies that came out in rapid-fire fashion. To add insult to injury, RBM was a micromanager's micromanager. She always looked over my shoulder. It got old rather quickly.

Vacation Time

The first policy change of the RBM administration affected vacation. We could not commit to vacation time unless it RBM approved it no greater than:

- a week in advance for 3 days of vacation or less, or
- a month in advance for a week of vacation or more

What? I had to plan more than a month in advance for vacation time of a week or more. Flights? Hotels? And for a long weekend, I couldn't confirm until a week out? This wasn't popular with anyone, as you'd imagine. I'd never had to ask permission for vacation in my 6 years at the company. I always managed backup coverage when I was out. I never had problems meeting my professional obligations before leaving.

Meetings and Extra Hours

Do you dislike meetings as much as I do, especially those that are unnecessary? RBM liked to use meetings as a show of power and to keep her team working late.

Specifically, she wanted to have a team meeting every day at 9 am and 6:30 pm. I told her that the evening meeting wouldn't work with my schedule and offered several late-afternoon alternatives. Her response was direct: "Group meeting at 6:30 p.m. is very critical for development team till March 18th. It will take 15 min. Please let me know the telephone number that I reach you at 6:30 pm."

I placed my next phone call to her manager, who tried unsuccessfully to moderate a solution. Basically, the evening call happened sporadically, dial-in details were seldom sent out, and when I did participate, I found I was not needed. I didn't lose any sleep over this.

RBM also said our performance would be assessed on our off-hours availability, outside of 8:30-5:30. She said working late was a virtue. She also stressed that we could refuse to work extra hours, though our performance rating would suffer if we weren't available for a late-night meetings or work. This was threatening to those of us who worked very hard during normal business hours to get our jobs done.

Travel & Trust

I traveled to the office for a few days each month, as had been my custom. RBM was really interested in my schedule while I was there. It was clear she wanted to make sure I was meeting with the right people, meeting enough people, and spending enough time with her. To that end, she asked me to "please send your meeting schedule at least two days prior to visits in future."

One 2-day trip was particularly difficult to plan. I wrote to ask permission to come to New York the following Tuesday and Wednesday. I gave her my proposed schedule. She responded that she needed me there the entire week. I looked at my schedule and countered that I could come Tuesday, Wednesday and Thursday. She immediately called me and told me it was critical I be there all week.

I'd sent her a note about an appointment on Monday. I also needed to be back home by 5 pm on Friday to leave for the weekend with my family. She offered that I could leave New York at 5 pm, putting me home at 10, and then said "I don't want to talk to you any more about this."

I persisted. After several more exchanges, she said the 3-day trip was fine. She asked for the schedule of my meetings. She told me she'd "fill in the rest of the time to meet with other people she sees fit." I pressed her for details. She said some of the meetings were for reviewing documents with her. I asked if she trusted me to review the documents by myself. She said of course, but she thought a joint review would help her understand the documents better.

Respect

RBM demonstrated a general lack of respect in communicating with the team. These vignettes are from that tumultuous spring of 2002.

RBM sent a directive via her administrator: "If you arrive in the office after 9 am or leave before 5 pm please send an email to me and cc: RBM regarding your whereabouts during this time." The times of day were not the problem; she didn't trust us to manage our own time. My colleagues weren't amused by this new attendance-taking policy, either. I half-hoped RBM would go as far installing a punch clock. I felt lucky to work remotely where I could not be judged by the minutes I was sitting at my desk. RBM had this message sent on the day her manager had surgery and would be out of the office for 4 weeks.

RBM terrorized individuals during her afternoon meetings. During one 5 p.m. session, RBM asked me about my progress on approving several design documents. I told her I had approved two and had six more in flight. RBM let a zinger rip: "You've approved the documents, but have you READ them?" The developers laughed. It was a relief to them that someone else was the target of RBM's barrage. I felt frustrated and defensive in the group setting and reiterated that I had indeed read them. RBM said to the group as solemnly as a preacher delivering a Sunday sermon, "Reviewing documents is something that needs to taken very seriously."

Finally, here's one last, most egregious example of RBM's disrespect for the team. A well-respected consultant made a suggestion that was at odds with RBM's opinion. The consultant's snack gave RBM the ammunition for a dehumanizing slight. She said the developer's name, paused, and said "Shut up and eat your banana."

RBM left our team shortly after that episode. I have to imagine that some of our collective criticism reached the right people. She then left the company after a period of languishing without a team.

Remember all the things that RBM did. Never — *ever* — treat people that way.

THAT'S JUST SICK (2003)

One of my managers never got sick. He was very proud of this. Whenever anyone around him showed a sign of being unwell, even an errant sneeze, he'd be there.

"You sick?"

"No," you'd reply. "It's just a runny nose."

He'd say, "I never get sick." Then he'd launch into all the myriad reasons for his wellness. This happened with the predictability of a Swiss train.

I'm sure he felt subpar sometimes, but it must have been on vacation, nights, or weekends. Perhaps he masked it well at work, coming in when he shouldn't have. Do some people never get sick? He seemed to be one of those super-healthy people that escapes flu season unscathed. I seem to have acquired some of his purported immunity as I've aged. I attribute most of that to environmental and lifestyle changes that are part of working remotely.

You can spot some recurring themes when you search for "how to get sick less often."

Exercise: Regular exercise is part of my weekly schedule. Before working remotely, I irregularly hit the gym to lift weights or play racquetball. I was mystified in college when my friends would go to the fitness center and use an elliptical or other cardio equipment for an hour. Now I routinely run 5+ times a week for at least that long. I enjoy weight-based group fitness classes that also serve as a social outlet. I run 5Ks, 10Ks, half marathons and ultra-marathons. I race at least one triathlon a year, which gets me on my bike and in the water to train. My lack of commute offers me many options to stay fit. Early mornings, late summer evenings, or the middle of the day: they all are workable. It's easy to start and end a run at my home where I can clean up quickly.

Hygiene: Communal bathrooms. Cubicle neighbors who spew germs in the air with every cough. Subway railings. Throngs of people in train and bus stations. Feeling sick yet? One study found that handrails on the New York subway offer you far more than stability. Hanging onto those subway railings gives you the bacterial equivalent of shaking hands with 10,000 people! Campaigning politicians don't even have that kind of exposure. I have far less risk at home with a wife and two kids. Our biggest risk is the kids bringing home a bug from school. When that happens, we get plenty of rest and emphasize good hygiene.

Diet: My family "eats a rainbow" and focuses on whole foods. Does it come in a bag or a box? You can't pronounce most of the ingredients? Then it's probably not as good for you as something from the produce section. We belong to a CSA (Community Supported Agriculture) farm so we get fresh produce most weeks of the year. We live near Wegmans, a grocery store we adore. They carry a wide variety of products and make it easy to steer clear of the junk we don't need. No matter your culinary preferences, variety and moderation are the keys to a healthy diet.

Rest: I've never regretted taking a day off work when I'm too sick to be productive. When I do get sick, I try going to bed earlier and taking it easy during the day. Bodies needs rest! I get 7-8 hours of sleep each night. I use Sleep Cycle for iOS to see how each night stacks up against my normal patterns and national averages.

Mindfulness and Relaxation: I've tried a few meditation apps to try to tune into my inner self, but it is not yet a habit. I enjoy practicing yoga and the inward focus it brings. I also schedule a monthly acupuncture treatment or massage. Those treatments help with aches and pains, if I have them, but they also relax me and center my mind. I look forward to these sessions and consider them an essential part of my fitness regimen. I set up a monthly reminder to schedule these appointments, though I don't know how I'd forget them!

We have an ongoing joke in my family about our primary care doctor. She's a very nice Chinese woman who was also my childhood doctor. My wife and I both see her when we have our annual checkups. We make ad-hoc appointments on the rare occasions that we get sick and recovery seems out of grasp. The doctor weighs us, talks to us about our symptoms, and takes other vital measurements. If she suspects the cause of our ailment is bacterial (which is rare), she gives us a prescription for antibiotics. Most of the time, though, we walk out with wisdom dispensed in the form of the "broken border" talk. Here's how it goes:

Your body is a village. Its border to the outside world is usually strong. But now, your defenses are down. Your border is broken. You are being invaded. You need strength to fight the invaders, and you need time to build up your defenses so invaders cannot get in. Take the time to lie down and rest. Do not work. Eat hot foods and drink hot drinks. Take warm baths and help your body fight the good fight.

We react the same way when she delivers the "broken border" talk. We chastise ourselves for rushing to the doctor when we should have taken care of ourselves. Oh, that copayment! There's Murphy's Law, though. If we didn't see her and it was bacterial, sickness could linger or progress into something worse. While we love seeing her, we now apply her suggestions before we make appointments. When we're not feeling 100%, we take proactive steps to fortify and defend our border.

I've also gone for long stretches without taking a sick day. This is one of the major benefits of remote work for employers and employees. Working remotely helps you get through minor colds without missing too much. Sickness doesn't have to derail you for an entire day. Same goes for medical and dental appointments: you don't need a full day off to take care of them when you work remotely.

If you're feeling lousy but you know you can still deliver on your commitments, work. If you're truly sick, take time off to get well. That's what sick days are for!

THE PATH LESS TRAVELED (2003)

I was rather surprised when a very senior manager wanted to have lunch with me during one of my business trips. I heard that he was leaving the company soon, so I thought it might be a kind of reverse exit interview. He managed Global Technology and interfaced with teams all over the world.

We ran the cafeteria gauntlet and found a quiet table. We chatted about work, where he was headed next, and other personal things. Then the conversation turned quite personal.

"Scott, I'm concerned about you." He folded his hands in front of him and smiled.

"Concerned? Why?"

He observed that I wasn't advancing as fast as my office-dwelling colleagues. He saw remote work as a limiting factor in my career path. I was touched that he took enough interest in my situation to have sought me out for this heart-to-heart. He put himself in my shoes and shuddered at my prospects. I didn't share his concerns.

I told him I had embraced remote work with my eyes wide open. I told him I was frustrated that geography limited my career growth.

I expressed how important work/life balance was to me. I talked to him about where I lived. We were almost finished building our home and my 3 year-old daughter would soon be joined by her brother. My parents already lived near the house we were building and my wife's parents would soon move nearby, too. As compensating factors go, the relative non-stress of small town living was huge.

I don't think Tim was sold. I believe he left that meeting confused that I wasn't more persuaded. We shook hands and went our separate ways. I liken it to an intervention — an attempt to course-correct my career. This intervention didn't work. I continued working remotely and he continued his management career through other companies. He was prescient, though. I did continue to experience his predicted stagnation in career growth. It wasn't due to my geography, though. It was because of the politics that affected everyone vying for promotion. I didn't put up with it for long, either. I found an even better remote working position and voted with my feet. I left.

Sadly, geography is still a limiting factor in promotion and advancement for remote workers. Unless you work for a fully-remote company, you've likely seen this in your workplace. It's an inequality that's unlikely to change as quickly as we'd like.

Working remotely has enabled me to have an incredible, rich, and reduced-stress life. I've had a wonderful relationship with my wife and helped my kids grow into well-adjusted teens. I built a home, kept up with fitness and health, and reconnected with my love of acting and music. I spent winters introducing my kids to alpine ski racing.

I wouldn't trade it for anything.

PERFECTION (2004)

As of this writing, I've worked for 18 different managers over my 22 year career. I learned something from each one of them. Some taught me things I'd emulate and adopt; others exhibited behaviors I avoid at all costs. Some lessons required a bit of processing, like this one.

I was on a short business trip to New York, and one of my meetings was an annual review with my manager. I sat in a guest chair inside the door of her small office. Her desk was between us as she shared my review.

I was eight years into my job at the company, six of them remote. I was getting jaded by corporate policies and procedures. The performance management cycle was particularly problematic for me. I always received high evaluations but I knew the grade was not linked to only my performance. It was linked to my performance as compared to others. You see, the company force ranked employees within departments. My department was small. Better ratings and compensation went to high performers deemed as "flight risks." The narrative feedback was seldom actionable and often predictable. I could almost write my own manager's comments!

You can't blame me for seeing performance reviews as a meaningless exercise.

My manager was mid-sentence when she sat up straighter, leaned toward me, and put her papers aside. She folded her arms on her desk and sighed.

"Why are you sitting like that?" she asked.

I snapped out of my reverie. "Like what?"

She continued, "All slouched in the chair, with your arm dangling like that."

Damn. I'd rarely been called on the carpet like that, but she was right. A white-hot sheet of embarrassment fell over my face. I adjusted myself in the uncomfortable chair so I was no longer slouching. I was ashamed for having been so relaxed. She was very serious. She then extemporaneously gave me the best feedback I've ever received in a review.

"You know what, Scott? You're too much of a perfectionist."

My shame and embarrassment turned to shock and anger. She gave me examples and suggestions to improve but I had stopped listening. I'm my own worst critic, but it cut deep to have someone else critique me that way. I'm a perfectionist? I kept rolling it over in my head but I could not accept it in the meeting. I was so taken aback by her bluntness. She could tell I disagreed. She asked me to think about it.

It took a few days but I came to see her point of view. I sent designs and documents out only when they were fully-baked — perfect, actually. My manager's point wasn't to let my standards slip too far. But far enough that I'd deliver something when it was good, not perfect. I had a reputation for getting things done. She knew that I could have a reputation for getting things done quickly. I've applied this principle since then. There's always time to iterate and improve. When I send something out for review, it's never perfect, but it's always good enough. I'm never embarrassed by the quality of something I deliver, but I know that I could do better. They're those grand variables in the productivity equation: time and effort! I short them just enough to get the feedback loop going as soon as possible. When you rush to perfection, you risk having to start over when you're on the wrong track.

That candid performance review was the beginning of an honest and open relationship. I took her feedback to heart. I first saw her as another manager in an organization that I was beginning to distrust. When she cared enough to speak up with some candid feedback, I saw her as someone who truly cared. I realized she was like me: a person with feelings, ambitions, goals, and fears. She cared enough to give me honest feedback. It came from a desire to help me, not to "check a box" and say we'd had a review. Her openness and honesty was refreshing. It turned out to be the start of one of the best manager relationships I've ever had.

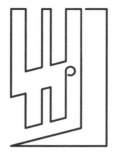

SHOULD I STAY OR SHOULD I GO (2013)

My career growth stalled after ten years. Despite my responsibilities growing, my compensation and title didn't. I was one of the leading user experience experts in the company. I managed a design team. I worked on every critical project. Heck, even the CTO referred to me as "our UX expert" in town hall meetings. What was going on?

I got insight into the problem when I had to fight for the ratings and compensation I felt my staff deserved. My department used a forced bell curve for ratings.

- 10% Superior Rock Star
- 15% Excellent Work
- 50% Oh-So-Politically-Correct "Meets Expectations"
- 15% Your Check Engine Light is On
- 10% You're Still Here?

Okay, so I made up the labels and percentages, but the spirit of the curve is here. Half the people are in the average bucket. Not good or bad. Meeting expectations! It's about as useful as giving someone a survey and having them mark the option right in the middle: "Neither agree nor disagree." It's frustrating to be on the receiving end of this! We'll come back to the bell curve, but in the meantime, that's why feedback in the form of commentary is golden. What have I done well? What can I improve upon? I can count on one hand the times I received actionable feedback in a performance review. Most of the time, though, my feedback was "keep doing what you're doing, you're doing great!" In that first 10-year period I always got one of the two highest ratings. It seemed like managers were free to give me a rating they felt I had earned. I'd be surprised if there was force ranking.

At some point the company started enforcing a forced bell curve distribution. I started receiving "Meets Expectations" ratings, yet my actual feedback had not changed. Same input, different output. My team had just six people. Senior managers asserted that the curve was applied at levels with hundreds of staff. My manager told me in private that this wasn't true. He was asked to rate his own group of six according to the bell curve. Three of us got the middle rating. Two received the excellent rating. One unlucky soul saw the proverbial "check engine light" blinking. Our group had been cut to the bone through staff reductions and reorganizations. The remaining six were a tight-knit collection of rock stars. My manager went into a conference room with his peers to make his case for exceptions to the curve. It was like some kind of perverse white-collar cage match. He was not successful.

My performance reviews started with "Well, you can see you have an average rating. I wanted to give you a higher rating, but that's how it came out." It turned into a defense of a perverted process instead of focusing on my performance. To add insult to injury, ratings affected compensation. I'd had it after a few years of stagnant ratings and compensation. I suspected higher ratings were going to flight risks. These were solid performers who management perceived as most likely to leave. I confirmed this when my manager involved me in the decision-making process. I was managing a part of the group that year. "Well, we can't lose Greg, can we?" he said. "So, we should give him the 2, and give the 3 to Sally." Greg and Sally's performance had no bearing on their rating and I could not defend these types of decisions. This is where remote work enters the equation. I was never deemed a flight risk in the negotiations. Management thought I was so lucky to work remotely that I couldn't (or wouldn't) walk across the virtual street and find a better deal. I was destined to get a 3 for the foreseeable future.

I focused my efforts on getting a title promotion. This would be a way around the bell curve. A title promotion was appropriate given my responsibilities. We were asked to "do more with less" and I was doing a great job as a manager and individual contributor. I asked my boss for a title promotion and he was encouraging. Several years passed with the same result. Same rating, same compensation, no title change. There was a new excuse for the lack of promotion, too. Now there were "too many middle managers." It wouldn't look good if they added me to a rather dense higher level of the organization chart. Like the curve, I was destined to stay in the middle. Not for any reason of demerit or lack of quality, but for bureaucracy.

It was time to go. I tapped my network and let people know I was looking around.

What can you do if you don't want to leave, though? You might find a similar forced curve where you work. Or, you may find a simple top-to-bottom ranking of employees. Your salary and bonus are totally contingent on where you fall in the list. As the Hamilton lyric goes, if you're in "the room where it happens" you'll see bargaining and negotiating of the placement of people in the list. Merit is not the only part of the bargaining equation, either. People move up and down based on whether they're likable, mission critical, or deemed a flight risk. Carla Harris gave a fantastic TED Talk that addresses this perfectly. You need a sponsor. No, it's not a mentor. It's an advocate. Someone who's in "the room where it happens" and will vouch for you when the time comes. Search for "Carla Harris" at ted.com and check out her talk titled "How to find the person who can help you get ahead at work." You'll be glad you did.

You always have a choice: stay or go. If you decide to go, be deliberate, never burn a bridge, and use your network.

Don't let someone make you feel that you're "lucky to have a remote job."

Do not accept treatment that's inconsistent with onsite peers.

Breaking Up and Moving Out (2013)

I was no longer being promoted despite receiving excellent written evaluations. I was also unsatisfied with my position in middle management. I enjoyed managing people but I wasn't producing anything on my own. I wasn't designing. I wasn't coding. I wasn't getting any recognition for my work. I was tired. It was time to break up and move out. It wasn't an easy decision. I'd been there 17 years but it was definitely time.

I didn't know where to start looking. I hadn't "looked for a job" since graduate school. I tapped my network. I was looking for a web design job where I could continue to work remotely. I was also looking for a salary commensurate with my experience. I had several interviews with headhunters who laughed at my salary requirements. They weren't outlandish — but they were higher than the sweet spot of the industry's salary bell curve. I kept at it, searching job listings and networking.

I met with local web design and development companies. I felt that a modest commute of 25 minutes wouldn't be too bad. It might even be positive to be in an office environment again! One company wasn't hiring but offered to send me freelance work. Another got cagey when they found out how long I'd been working at one company. I also had a video interview with a university, but that's where that lead stopped. I think many companies were scared off by my tenure. They wanted younger college graduates they could more easily mold into their cultures.

I came very close to working for a startup in California. One of the founders was someone I met during my first days in the associate program. The job sounded perfect and they were willing to let me work remotely. We were sorting out salary vs. equity when I received terrible news. The board wasn't comfortable with a remote employee. They asked if I could work in San Jose. It was like a sucker punch to the gut. I knew this would be incompatible with my life. My kids were 9 and 12. The salary was not enough for my family to live on if we moved to the area. I'd miss so much of the next few years and spend a ton of time and money traveling back to see them. I passed on the opportunity.

My search came to a close with one of my former managers. He was a senior manager at a financial services company on Wall Street. The company was operated by two private equity firms. My former manager knew I had the chops to work remotely. He could guarantee remote work as a condition of the web design job. During an initial phone interview, the development manager introduced a potential hitch. The team was small and they couldn't take on a full-time designer. They needed someone who could design part-time and also write code. Was I that person? I have subscribed to Lynda.com for a long time. I took courses for my nights-and-weekends freelance work and personal projects. Yet, I never learned anything I couldn't apply to another side project or my day job. I passed the company's front-end development technical interview. Continuous learning to the rescue!

I traveled to New York to interview for the hybrid designer/ developer role. I conducted an expert review of the team's website in advance. I balanced respect for their decisions with showing how things could be improved. The website I'd work on was new and very much a part of the company's strategic direction. The team was small and operated as a startup within a far larger company. Since it was funded by private equity, though, the funding was not as limited as a startup. It was bureaucracy-free but not resource-free. I was sold.

I received their offer and negotiated my salary — a modest bump from my current compensation. They needed me to start as soon as I could. I thought I would be able to have a week or two between jobs to reset, but that was not to be. I planned to stop work at the bank on a Friday and start at the new job on Monday. My two-week notice period flew by. I worked into the mid-afternoon of my last day, said my goodbyes, and logged out of my computer for the last time. As I walked out of my house to see my family on that sunny June afternoon, I felt something I hadn't felt in a long time. It was a feeling of freedom, of being unencumbered by commitments to an employer. It was wonderful to have this feeling for two days. Does freelancing bring with it similar feelings, when you're your own boss? Perhaps I'll find out someday when both of my kids are off to college.

I spent the next week meeting my new team in New York and configuring my laptop for development work. It was stressful at the time, but only because I was learning a new culture and development stack. The technology setup was even better than what I was accustomed to. Instead of a virtual machine, I got an encrypted laptop that was mine to configure. They issued me an IP phone that would work anywhere in the world. My colleagues could dial my 6-digit extension and it'd ring in my home office. I got my own WebEx account for collaboration. We all were on the same instant messaging platform. I could use open-source software without going through a cumbersome approval process. They were right about the lack of bureaucracy: everything was seamless.

The first few months in my new job validated my decision to change companies. It was a happier place. I honed my front-end development skills. I was an individual performer again! It was satisfying to create something valuable almost every day. I enjoyed designing, getting business approval, and bringing those designs to life.

Yes, breaking up and moving out was a very good decision. You can walk across the virtual street and find a better deal. I know. It's possible.

Grow and cultivate your network. You never know who can help you blaze your career path.

The Art of Working Remotely

II: The Space

How can you set up an effective work area? What infrastructure will you need? What about office pets? What should you wear? How can you keep from raiding the pantry? Read on.

WORKSPACE

Find a space where you can focus with few disruptions. This might be a home office or part of another room where you'll have privacy during work hours. I've had the pleasure of working remotely from four places so far.

Waltham, Massachusetts (1998): I moved from Long Island to Waltham when I started working remotely. The apartment had three bedrooms: one for work, one for painting and crafts, and one for sleeping. I could have saved by renting a 2-bedroom instead, setting up in the corner of our bedroom or our living room since my wife taught all day. It wasn't that loud when she was home, after all! The office looked out over a small courtyard outside our door where we had a bistro table and some plants.

Speaking of plants, we still laugh about this story: we bought some indoor plants to liven up the space, and since I was home during the day I thought it'd be nice for the plants if I gave them some more sun on nicer days. I took them outside and left them for hours at a time. They wilted, struggled to survive in the heat, and acquired an infestation of small bugs. I've been working since then on my green thumb!

Scott Dawson

Fairport, New York (1999): Things were different when we moved to New York. We were starting a family! We rented a townhouse with three bedrooms: one for work, one for a nursery, and one for sleeping. This arrangement was ideal since I had a quiet place to focus and make phone calls.

Trumansburg, New York (2002): We lived in a 2-bedroom apartment in Trumansburg while waiting for our house to be built. The landlord kept loud dogs in their adjacent unit. My wife stayed home with our 2 year-old daughter. I needed a quieter place to work! My childhood home was nearby and it was empty during the day since my parents were both still working. I'd have my first "commute" in four years! Yes, it was weird to take conference calls and build wireframes in my childhood bedroom. I got over it, though, and the arrangement worked well.

Trumansburg, New York (2003): I designed my home office for remote work. The room is upstairs and out of the way. It has extra insulation in the floor and interior walls to help keep noise levels down. Most importantly, it has a door. Outside the door is a small sitting area with Amy's computer. Beyond the sitting area is the only other room on the second floor. It started out as a craft room but we've since converted into a commercial kitchen for Amy's bakery.

There's a lot to consider when setting aside a space to work in your home. I'm happy with most everything we did to create a quiet space. The home office does double-duty, too: it's a media room and place to relax in the evening. We furnished it with a comfortable couch, a television, and a separate table for work and play.

Door

A door is your first line of defense against disruptions. I love to keep mine open to circulate air and have a more open feel. I close it when anyone's home and I need to focus or make a phone call. The closed door is a signal that I'm busy. My family knows they can interrupt me if the door is open, but they have to be more cautious if it's closed. If you have small kids, it might be fun to have them help make a busy/free sign for the door. It could be like the "Do Not Disturb" door knob hangers in hotels. If they help make it they may be more likely to understand what it means!

Lighting

It's nice to have a window. Natural light can elevate your mood — it feels good to look outside while you're working. When the kids were young I watched them play on the swing set in the backyard. Now that we've replaced the swing set with a garden, I can look out at all the things growing there. I wouldn't fare well in a basement office without a window, or with a narrow sliver of one. I was fortunate to have a window cubicle when I got my first job in New York City. Most of the cubicle-dwellers on the floor weren't as lucky.

You'll also need good lighting at your workspace. In the depths of winter I start working as the sun comes up and quit after it gets dark. I have a good desk lamp for task lighting and some nice general lighting for the room.

Desk or Table

There are so many options for work surfaces! It's a personal decision, so take some time to find what'll work best for you. Traditional desks and tables are simple to try out. You might also try out standing desks and treadmill desks. I started out with a glass-topped desk with steel legs in my home office. I had to work at a normal desk height, but I liked the aesthetic of it more than anything.

I flirted with the idea of a standing desk and recently invested in one. I found a way to keep my glass-topped desk in the office, too, which made me feel better about the decision. If you search for "convert normal desk to a standing desk" you'll find plenty of off-the-shelf and do-it-yourself options.

Treadmill desks have slow-moving treadmills with a desktop set at the proper height. Manufacturers tout benefits of improved mood, reduced stress, and the calorie burn from walking as you work.

Chair

Your chair, like your work surface, is such a personal choice. The options are a bit mind-boggling:

- a simple no-frills chair
- office chair
- executive chair
- Aeron chair
- inflatable ball
- kneeling chair
- reclining chair
- saddle chair
- … a myriad of other options!

You need a comfortable seat that gives you good support and promotes good posture.

Research ergonomics and posture before you buy. Examine how the chair can adjust your body's position relative to your desk. I sat in a cheap traditional office chair for a long time but found that I leaned against the back too much. My back was paying the price so I switched to an inflatable ball chair. It forces me into a better posture since there's no back to lean on. You may not need a chair at all if you stand to work, either. Standing stools are also popular if you need to take a sitting break at a standing desk without changing the desk height. I also struggled with wrist position and tension earlier in my career. A comfortable mouse pad with a gel wrist rest fixed that problem.

Ambiance

Of the ironies I encounter while traveling, a bland office sticks out the most. I meet with a lot of managers surrounded by cookie-cutter desks and credenzas. These bland pieces of furniture are adorned with the sparest of personal touches. The walls are eggshell white. Bookshelves are spattered with topical reference books and tchotchkes. I'd go nuts if I had to work each day in that environment!

There's so much you can do to make a space "yours" whether it's at home or in an office. Start with color on the walls. Paint them with colors you enjoy. Hang things that are meaningful and inspirational: posters, paintings, maps, photos, or designs. My office has a map of the Erie Canal, from a top-down traditional view and an elevation view. I was so inspired by the creativity of the map maker that I thought it'd be a brilliant addition to the office. I have another larger map that shows the depths of the Finger Lakes where I live. I also have an oil painting my wife created and some pictures of local waterfalls.

Items from a movie or TV series you enjoy can be fun, too. Movie posters are easy to come by and desk-sized characters from Funko Pop are super fun. Add some plants (don't forget to water them) for some extra texture and color. Place books that you love to refer to on your bookshelf. Orient your favorites with the cover facing out.

If you enjoy ambient sounds while you work, check out apps like brain.fm, Noisli, and Coffitivity.

Distractions

You have your room with a door, a place to sit, and some fantastic ambiance. Great! You'll still be nowhere if you don't cut distractions, though. They come in many forms!

It can be difficult to have a single computer since it's so easy to switch between leisure and work tasks. I have two computers on my desk: one for personal use and one for my full-time job. I like to sleep my personal computer during the day so I'm not distracted by alerts and notifications. Conversely, my work laptop is asleep evenings and weekends so I'm not tempted to check work email. If you have a single device, it may support multiple desktops or profiles. Set up your screens based on your task flow and you'll cut down on distractions.

Try keeping track of your time. You might change productivity-draining habits by raising your level of awareness. There are tons of time trackers for billing purposes. RescueTime has been mentioned several times in conversations with other remote workers. It tracks "time spent on applications and websites, giving you an accurate picture of your day." As of iOS 12, Apple devices aggregate usage reports in Settings > Screen Time. You can set scheduled downtime, limit usage, and identify apps that take up most of your time.

It may work well to change your location based on what you're doing. I wrote this book on my iPad Pro during a half-hour period each morning. I usually sat at our dining room table or kitchen counter and I didn't open any other apps until time was up. I grabbed my morning coffee, set a timer for a half hour, and wrote! No distractions. Having a specific place to work helps reinforce good productivity habits. Having a routine minimizes the chance you'll get derailed by distractions.

Multitasking is the mother of all distractions. Your attention is pulled from task to task, and both tasks can suffer. The following tips may help you stay focused on one thing at a time:

- Set a timer. Don't stop working on a task until the time is up.

- Commit to completing one task before switching to another. Better yet, promise yourself a "reward" — like going for a walk, running an errand, or refilling your coffee — when a task is complete.

- Move to another location, like another room or a coffee shop, and set a goal to complete the task before you get up again.

- Declutter your workspace. If you're looking at something else in your periphery you're not focused on your task. Get rid of visual reminders that you have other things to do.

- Turn off your phone's notifications and place it face down. Better yet, use airplane mode.

- Shut down any other apps on your computer that may distract you.

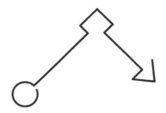

INFRASTRUCTURE

Remote workers are likely working in the information economy. The tools of the trade don't depend much of your specific role. There are many resources to help you choose the best tools. Research what will work best for your own situation.

Internet

You need a high-speed Internet connection. ISDN (128 Kbps!) was state-of-the-art when I started working remotely. Now I have a cable connection with over 100 Mbps. Oh, how times have changed, but needs have changed, too! We live in a world with cloud computing, massive data files, streaming video, Internet phones, and videoconferencing. These bandwidth-hungry beasts demand a high-speed Internet connection.

I've been with the same Internet provider for many years and recently asked if I could have my bill reduced. They told me I was using one of their outdated modems. Upgrading would reduce my bill and jump me from 10 Mbps to 100 Mbps. Reach out to your provider if it's been a while since you've talked with them. With the fast pace of technology change, you may find a deal waiting for you!

Voice

This section titled used to be "phone" but when I thought more about it, it's not quite the right label. When you speak with someone else, it may be through a phone. It's also likely to be through software on a computer or device. Regardless of the path your voice takes, make sure your voice quality is as good as possible. It's one of the impressions you make when you're working remotely. You don't want to be the person with the horrible voice connection.

When I started my current job, I had a Voice-Over-IP phone that my colleagues also used in their offices. I plugged it into my home network and it appeared as if I was in the New York City office. I could be halfway around the world yet all one had to do was dial my 6-digit extension. I coupled this with a wireless headset and it was perfect.

When the company upgraded their phones they asked me to use a software-based phone. I could place and receive calls from my laptop or an app on my phone. I tried both and neither was ready for prime time. The voice quality was poor and the usability of the apps was horrible. I opted to use my cell phone instead, the caveat being that my office extension was now defunct. At least with the cell phone I can walk away from my desk on longer conference calls!

I recently won an Amazon Echo and was delighted that it had calling features. The speaker's clarity is great and I've found it ideal to use for conference calls and direct calls to colleagues. There are a few easily-countered drawbacks. First, there's no button to disconnect the call. Instead of saying "Alexa, end my call" if others are still dialed in, I have to unplug the unit. There's no way to enter numbers after you dial the main number. Connecting to a conference call with a code seemed impossible. I found a free DTMF (dual-tone multi-frequency) generator app that solves the problem. You can hold it up near the speaker and generate the tones you need. Search for "DTMF dialer" and you'll find what you need.

Regardless of what you use, use your mute button like a pro. I've had several mishaps where I thought I was on mute, but was not. Others shouldn't have to talk over your neighbor's leaf blower, kids yelling, dishes clanging, or (gasp) sounds from the bathroom. Don't we all have a story like that? Don't make that mistake.

Video

Videoconferencing seems to be a part of the culture for some companies. My company doesn't use it but I know plenty of remote-only companies that do. I enjoy chatting with other remote workers over video. It enhances the quality of the communication.

I tried to use video shortly after starting my current job. I was in a conference room where a WebEx was being presented to several remote participants. One of the remote participants was on the team that hired me and he joined via video. "Excellent," I thought, "videoconferencing is culturally accepted here!" I bought a USB camera for my laptop. I used it once during a meeting with my immediate team and, since nobody else was using video, it was pretty weird.

Whether it is over Skype, Zoom, Google Hangout or something else, collaboration over video is the wave of the future. It just hasn't arrived for me yet!

Printer and Scanner

I remember when the term "paperless office" was popular. Everything was going to be digital and we wouldn't need printers, scanners and fax machines. We're getting there. I print a lot less than I used to. I prefer to print and read longer documents offline. There's something about sitting in a different space with a colored pen to annotate in the margin. When I'm done, I transcribe those notes back into the document at my desk. I also use my printer for one-off things like printing off a web page to bring with me somewhere (concert tickets, anyone?).

I bought a personal scanner from Doxie. It's great for scans that need to be high-quality as you can control the DPI and color settings. For quick scans (and most are) I use TurboScan. Device cameras have come a long way and it's so convenient. TurboScan takes three pictures of your document and creates a crisp, cropped PDF or image. When you're done, you can sync or send it anywhere. For personal editing, my wife and I use ForScore to import documents on our iPads, mark them up digitally, and re-export as PDFs. It's a pretty great way to edit without the bulk of a physical printout!

Laptop or Desktop

I wrote this book on an iPad Pro, a tablet that's almost ready to be a laptop replacement. Almost. Depending on the type of work you're doing, you may need the full functionality of a laptop or the power of a desktop. Additionally, extra screen real estate can be such a nice productivity enhancement. You can have more windows open and visible, easing the transition through a workflow. Hardware is such a personal choice! I have an iMac for my home use and an external monitor hooked up to a Windows laptop for my day job. My company requires encryption and a VPN connection from a company-owned laptop. I don't have dual monitors, but other than that I'm pretty happy with the setup.

Backup Services

Save your work! Backup your data! How many people do this? It only took a few lost documents for me to be vigilant about where I save my work and how often I save it. I don't think these problems will plague the next generation as much with the advent of cloud computing. Now that you've saved your work, think about hard drive failure or a catastrophe (fire, flood or theft). Cloud services have backups of backups so a catastrophic loss of data is less likely. At home, though, you have gigabytes of files, pictures and videos on various media. What's your strategy for retaining these? I tried a cloud backup service to store everything from my drive but that got too costly (and slow!) and I didn't see the benefit.

I use 1 TB USB drives to counter hard drive failure. They're relatively cheap and you can use software to selectively backup files. If there were a fire or flood it's easy to grab these portable drives and run. It's not perfect, though, since tragedy can strike when you're not home. That's why we store most of our music, photos, videos and documents in the cloud. Hard drives are a secondary backup option.

We subscribe to Apple Music for a monthly fee. Similar subscription models are available from Amazon, YouTube, Google, Pandora, and Spotify (among others). I can access any music I like and the music I already owned is accessible from any device. There's no need to back any of this up.

We have a ton of photos to sift through each month, thanks to our family's four photographers. I go through them monthly in iPhoto and delete blurry shots and duplicates. Of those, I choose the most memorable to upload to Flickr. At the end of each year, I make a montage (12 photos) for each of my kids. If all we had left was our Flickr account and the monthly pictures, we wouldn't shed a tear. We don't have offsite backups of iPhoto but the library is backed up to the 1TB drive.

Our videos used to languish in iMovie. We published some on YouTube but most others were left unused. I started getting nervous about our volume of video data so I came up with an approach to keep only what we needed. I uploaded everything we wanted to keep to Vimeo, bought a subscription that would meet our storage and upload needs, and set most family videos to be private. A lot of our family videos are not in the public interest. When we shoot new video — most often on our phones — we edit it, upload it and delete the original. We're not movie-makers who need the raw video and Vimeo allows us to download 1080p if we need it. Storing videos online does double-duty, too. Sure, they're retained in case of catastrophe, but our family can also enjoy the videos on our AppleTV. No more gathering digital dust while they sit on our desktop!

We keep important documents in several cloud-based services. It's great to be able to sync them to other devices and know they're protected in case of a catastrophe. We use Apple Notes and the free versions of Google Drive and Dropbox. We also use Trello for a few things that need collaboration. I wrote this book in a Google Doc. It gave me the flexibility to write in my office, outside, or at the dining room table with the iPad. It's nice to not be tethered based on where your data is stored.

Backup Power

My neighbor's generator comes to life and keeps their lights on when the power goes out. This can happen quite often when severe thunderstorms roll through my area. I was jealous for awhile until I priced out generators. Expensive! I used to have backup power supplies for our desktops. They helped avoid surges and provided parachute power as computers shut down.

When they started failing (and alarming loudly) in the middle of the night, I decided it wasn't that important. Power outages are less impactful now that we have laptops and tablets. Our desktops don't have trouble rebooting after a power outage and they're plugged into surge-suppressing power strips.

Your situation may be different, requiring ample backup power, but it's nice to not need it. You don't have to have wi-fi or power to get work done, either. If the power goes out, there are a lot of things you can do. Read, organize your workspace, brainstorm, work in offline mode (if you've set that up on your laptop or device), or call a colleague. It may be time to step away from the desk and recharge your own batteries, too. Break out the candles, put the food in a cooler and go for a walk. The power, after all, will come on again.

Mobility

It's tough to sit most of the day. Commuting at least forces you to walk — to your office building or to and from your car, train or plane. As a remote worker without a commute, it's important to stand and move around. My office is on the second floor so I get a trip down and up the stairs when I refill my coffee or use the bathroom.

Even if your schedule is jam-packed with meetings, grab a few minutes to go for a quick walk. Can't get away? Take a call from your cell phone or headset so you can be mobile. It feels so good to move around instead of sitting around a conference table for an entire hour (or more). That's what you'd be doing if you were in a traditional office! Make sure you know how to mute your phone. There's nothing worse that unintended background noises on a call! We've all made this mistake at one point or another and it's a hard lesson to learn.

If you are stuck at your desk, try chair yoga or dynamic stretching. I have stretching exercises that I sometimes do while I'm on conference calls. It can be easier to actively listen when I'm doing something like that instead of multitasking. I know, multitasking is tempting when you're dialed into a meeting! However, it's so annoying to have a huge lead-up to a question and the target says, "Oh, I'm sorry, I wasn't paying attention." I hear this often, even from people who are calling in from a traditional office.

If you encounter a problem you can't solve, get up and move around. When I'm spinning my wheels I like to put the problem aside and go for a run, bike or hike. I come back with the solution, or several approaches that might lead to the solution. My wife bakes in a commercial kitchen in our home and she also takes strategic breaks. When the weather is nice in the summer we take a full hour and go for a "loop walk" after lunch. Our neighborhood has a loop we can walk in 20 minutes. It's a great way to get in some moderate midday exercise and catch up with my spouse.

While we're on the topic of fitness, it's nice to work for a company that embraces remote work. Before my current company merged with another, they reimbursed employees for $600 of annual fitness-related expenses. They offered this to everyone — remote or not — and I used it to defray the cost of my gym membership. 37 Signals, a remote-friendly company that was the birthplace of BaseCamp and Ruby on Rails, offers their employees $100 per month for a health club membership. They also pay for a weekly Community Supported Agriculture subscription (signalvnoise.com/posts/3151). Healthy eating could be a chapter of its own, but I can summarize it here. If you get fresh fruits and vegetables in your front door, you'll be more likely to eat them!

You don't have to stay in one spot all day long, either. Some remote workers are home in the morning and at a traditional office in the afternoon. You're not stuck in your home office for the entire day. You can enjoy a total change in scenery for the morning, afternoon, or the whole day! Don't be afraid to get out if you need to. There are probably a few WiFi-friendly coffee shops or coworking spaces a reasonable distance from your home. A change of scenery can inspire you, and you may befriend others in similar situations. There are some great websites that can help you locate potential places to set up shop for the day.

When you're remote, connect to wifi hotspots you know and trust. Open networks can be used by hackers so be deliberate when choosing a network to join. Larger companies like Starbucks, Barnes & Noble, Panera and McDonald's have free wifi locations nationwide. You can also check wififreespot.com or specialty iOS and Android apps that help you find wifi. Looking for coworking spaces? Check out workfrom.co and coworker.com. Most coworking spaces will also give you a free day pass to try it out. It never hurts to ask!

CLOTHING

It's not cited often enough, but wardrobe flexibility is one of the biggest benefits of working remotely. I spent my entire career in finance. Business casual is all the rage on Fridays, and only then if you're in a non-client location. Since working remotely, the "formal wear" section of my closet has dwindled.

I used to own five suits, many dress shirts, and tons of accessories. I spent a lot of spare time ironing my shirts and sometimes splurged on dry cleaning. After 20 years of working remotely I'm down to two ill-fitting suits and a few dress shirts. I can't remember the last time I had to dress up! My current company is all business casual so packing to travel is simple. The only other time I wear business casual is to "dress up" to attend a school play, concert, or special night out. I haven't spent money on work clothes in years.

Let's assume you spend $100 per month on your professional appearance. It might take you 3+ hours each month to select and buy things. Since we're talking about a huge variety of clothing, this is still a conservative estimate. The shopping list is long, considering the options across genders: suits, ties, scarves, shirts, dresses, skirts, pantsuits, undershirts, bras, tights, socks, shoes, and accessories. We're only talking about clothing here, too, not grooming or cosmetics. It'll cost $1,200 and 36 hours of time to buy clothing each year. That's airfare for two and spans a full week of productivity. And let's face it, all this shopping is happening on company time. I've seen it during business travel in meetings. Attendees have one browser tab open on Nordstrom and another on the document we're reviewing.

To be clear, I don't think I have a net savings by not having a professional wardrobe. I spend money differently. I buy workout clothes, running shoes, leisure clothing, and fund my family's downhill skiing habit. Does spending money this way bring me far more joy? Yes! I live in a small village of about 2,000 people and I characterize the wardrobe of the area as "Trumansburg chic." I shop for groceries wearing clothes that might look out of place in a bigger city. "Dressing up" for a dinner out means jeans, a t-shirt, and since I'll be wearing shoes — socks. I deliver my wife's baked goods to an organic grocery store several mornings each week. I wear workout shorts, a tech shirt, and a pair of beat-up Crocs. The tread is gone and their original white turned a weary shade of gray. I wear these things because they're the simplest to put on in the morning. I don't turn many heads dressing this way because nobody seems to care. I don't care. It's liberating to wear what makes you comfortable!

After the bakery delivery I stay in workout clothes (if I'm running right away) or put on jeans or shorts and a shirt. The key point is this: don't go to work in your pajamas. Put on something that makes you comfortable but signals you're awake! It doesn't require much thought and it's not unlike Steve Jobs' approach to clothing. He always wore a black mock turtleneck, blue jeans, and New Balance sneakers. He didn't waste much brain power in the morning choosing what he'd wear. I much prefer to save my brainpower — and my money and my time — for more enjoyable pursuits!

FOOD

If your work day involves a meal time (most likely lunch), take the time to enjoy it. It's important to reset and think about something different, if only for a few minutes. Throughout my career I've seen people forego a solid midday break. How many of you have seen (or done) these things?

- Skip lunch only to be starving by mid-afternoon and unable to focus
- Eat at a conference table during a meeting
- Eat at a desk alone while continuing to work

In any of the above scenarios, they were not fully present for the joy of eating or the mindfulness (or is it mindlessness?) of the meeting they were attending. You may have to eat at your desk sometimes — taking bites between microbursts of work — but those should be the exception, not the rule.

I put a daily appointment titled "Lunch" in my work calendar. It's a great prompt for me to take the time for a relaxing lunch. More importantly, it usually prevents anyone from scheduling meetings that conflict with it. It works most of the time! There are so many ways to use a midday hour when you work remotely. My wife is home with me most summer days: we prepare a quick lunch, enjoy it together, and read a book or go for a short walk. My very favorite days of the year are warm summer days. We enjoy a generous salad on our deck with birds chirping in the backyard and the sun warming our backs. Then we walk around our neighborhood together. It is so nice to connect with someone, share stories and return to work rejuvenated. When I'm alone for the day, I still take a break. Lunch is usually prepared in advance. Eating is quick, freeing me to play guitar or do some light yard work before returning to the office.

Now, on to snacking. How do you handle such ready access to food when it's not time for a meal? I struggle with this daily! I run a lot and my body seems to cry for calories non-stop. A lot of people working remotely — runners or not — struggle with this. It's so easy to open the pantry or refrigerator door and see what's available. How can you avoid grazing throughout the day?

I try to commit to having two snacks during the day — mid-morning and mid-afternoon. Planning in advance can help me ignore the temptation to graze. I usually have cottage cheese, yogurt with homemade granola, or an apple with peanut butter. On decadent days I enjoy a cookie from my wife's bakery. The snack is not a meal, so don't prepare a loaded platter of nachos!

I weigh myself on a smart scale every morning. My goal is to maintain a steady weight. It's easier to talk myself out of having extra food when I see my weight start to fluctuate. Here are some other ideas to minimize snacking:

- Three square meals a day — when it is a meal time, eat enough. Start your day off with an adequate breakfast, pack or buy enough for lunch, and enjoy a healthy dinner. Try to keep your meal times as constant as possible.

- Grab a cup of coffee, tea or water instead of food. Your hunger may really be thirst and can be satisfied with something to drink.

- Distract yourself by doing something different. A short-term task, a quick game on your phone or a short walk may help. Your hunger could really just be boredom!

- Don't stock your pantry and refrigerator with things you shouldn't eat. Don't go grocery shopping when you're hungry, either! We use a list each time we go shopping so our house doesn't have a ton of snack options that are bad for us. Instead, we have a bowl full of fruit on the dining room table, a container of homemade granola and yogurt in the fridge, and a package of trail mix in the pantry.

COMPANIONS

I can't believe I worked from a home office for so long without an office pet. Most of my remote work time has been pet-free! My remote peers around the world share about their many pets. Dogs, cats, birds, turtles, rabbits and others keep us happy throughout the day.

Snowball was a Florida White rabbit. He was pure white with red eyes. His breed is generally docile, gentle, and good-natured. He was such a great companion! He was a classroom pet when he was younger. He left school to live in the teacher's home after the kids were a bit rough with him, though. The teacher got pregnant and tried to find him a good home. The only pet experience we had were raising aquatic frogs from Brookstone. My kids begged to have a rabbit! My wife reminded me that she had rabbits when she was growing up in Germany. We visited Snowball to see if we'd be interested.

We welcomed him into our home a few days later. We set up his litter box, cage, hay, food and water in our craft room. He was litter trained so we wouldn't be spending all our time cleaning up! I built a small gate for the doorway and made sure the room was bunny-proofed. Bunny-proofing is like childproofing to the nth degree. You have to keep a keen eye out for things that can be chewed. His cage door was always open, and he spent most of his time hopping on the hardwood floor and exploring the room.

He enjoyed the room but he still made quite a mess. We had to clean the floor a lot! He seemed happy being able to roam, though, and we loved having him hop around our legs and letting us hold him. He bonded closely with my daughter. She's the only one he trusted to hold him for extended periods of time. She was the official nail-trimmer for this very reason.

After a year of so in the craft room, we planned to move my wife's Emoticakes business into that room. Her bakery needed a commercial 3-bay sink, oven, prep tables, mixers and ingredients. It wouldn't be a good place for a hairy bunny, despite his amiable nature. I thought about what it'd be like to have him in my office. My office already did triple-duty as a media room and guest room with a pull out couch. It was carpeted, too. How would it handle Snowball's periodic messiness? What about all the hair? There weren't many other options, though, so I threw myself into bunny-proofing my office.

I used an old legless train table I made for the kids as a place for Snowball's things. The trains had long since been put away. I added a plastic liner to hold his litter box, water, hay, and food. It would also help contain some of his messiness (his little feet tend to kick around detritus). I tied up the cords behind the entertainment center and moved them up out of reach. My printer stand served double-duty: the top shelf concealed the wifi router and printer cords and the lower shelf was a quiet place for Snowball. I covered the mouth of the bottom shelf entrance with some remnant fabric. The cable nest under my desk was a logistical issue. There were a lot of cords and power strips for the computers and accessories. I bought flat sheets of clear rigid plastic online. They made the perfect enclosure to keep the cords clear of Snowball's curiosity. The door gate I built for the craft room ported to my office door.

I stepped back and admired my handiwork. The room looked the same, but was now rabbit-proof! Snowball moved in and seemed quite happy to explore. His little paws found purchase on the carpeted surface and he hopped around happily. He was home!

Sharing the office was wonderful for both of us: we each had a constant companion during weekdays. The room was easy to keep tidy since his supplies were contained in the corner. I cleaned his litter and freshened his food and water every morning before breakfast. Some mornings he'd get a bowl of lettuce or a carrot. Since I was in the room all the time, errant bunny waste (there isn't much) got picked up quickly. Snowball changed his coat at least twice a year. I could tell when it started since the office became inundated with fur. Luckily I'm not allergic and the whole family took turns brushing him.

Rabbits are crepuscular — they're most active at dusk and dawn. Snowball hopped around enthusiastically when we greet ed him in the morning, begging us to come and say hello. Sometimes I have to provide off-hours support for work in the middle of the night. He was SO active at 2 a.m.! Most of the day, though, he was rather chill. He had favorite spots where he set up shop for hours at a time. My most favorite time was during winter when he's at my feet. That's the epitome of cozy.

I never thought an office pet could change my mood so much, but it did. I could take a break when I was stressed, get down on his level, and pet him between the ears. When he was happy he'd subtly grind his teeth. He was the very picture of peace when I pet him — settling in for the duration, chomping and grinding his teeth as his eyelids grew heavy.

We sadly had to say goodbye to Snowball in January, 2019. It was heart wrenching to say goodbye to my friend, and I wrote this on Facebook to let my friends know what had happened:

My heart is broken today. This morning we said goodbye to Snowball. It was nearly impossible to be a Dad to my children when my own heart was shattered, just as it was when I said goodbye to pets in my own childhood. I'll be forever grateful to have known this little bunny. He shared my office, taught my family lessons about love, and showed us that yes, rabbits can swim. He was so happy here, and we miss him dearly. Goodbye, Snowball. Rest in peace, little one.

Snowball outlived his life expectancy by at least a year or two. I think he owed this in no small part to being in a relatively stress-free, open environment. Turns out that he, too, had found one of the benefits of working remotely! I missed my co-worker, but took some solace in the fact that we'd given him such a happy life.

Six days later, my wife and kids saw that the SPCA in Tompkins County had a rabbit up for adoption. They begged to go see her. Not to adopt, mind you. Just to pet her. To hold her. Yeah, right. I got a phone call shortly after they got there.

My wife said, "She's really cute. What do you think about having another office pet?"

Phoebe came into our lives that afternoon. I have to admit, it's nice having a friend in the office again. She's so different from Snowball in many ways, and we've had to get to know each other and do more bunny-proofing. In the end, though, it's 100%

worth the work and the minor stress of introducing a new pet into our house.

Yes, office pets rule! If you find one that will enhance your work experience, go for it.

III: THE HABITS

How can you manage remote teams and be a good remote employee yourself? What is good communication and how can you promote transparency with what you're working on? What are the key habits employers are looking for in remote employees?

These are some behaviors and practices that can contribute to remote worker success.

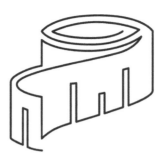

MEASUREMENT

It's important to measure things, whether you work for yourself or for a company. Peter Drucker said "you can't manage what you can't measure." Actually, you can't do a lot of things if you don't measure them. Keep track to help you plan your marketing, budgeting, and time management. You've heard of the 80/20 rule, right? It's also known as the Pareto Principle, after Italian economist Vilfredo Pareto. Pareto worked with real estate and pea pods, but his principle has been applied to business, science, software, and sports. In business, you may find that 80% of your profits come from 20% of your clients. The goal of measuring is to identify the 80 and the 20. Then, focus on trimming, delegating, automating, or ditching the rest.

One of the measurements I make as a developer is to track how many commits I make to our version control system. I have an email rule that puts a receipt of the commit in a special folder. I also send my team a "weekly wrap" email on Fridays with my key accomplishments. At yearly evaluation time, I comb through these emails and identify the impact I've had. It's easy to come up with a total number of commits and a bulleted list of major initiatives. I'm always surprised by the volume of things I accomplish in a year and it's fun to look back and recall what I did.

At review time, remember that numbers mean everything to managers. If you're working for yourself, retaining key metrics can help you identify trends. The way you measure and track things is less important than the act of doing it. You can use a notebook or a Google Sheet, Excel or email — it doesn't matter, as long as it works for you! You might consider tracking:

- Income and expenses (a table-stakes measurement for tax time)
- Client satisfaction (surveys)
- Time tracking per client, per project
- Orders per client
- Revenue per client
- Support costs per client
- Time to resolve client issues
- Repeat purchases or engagements
- Lines of code committed
- Illustrations drawn per month
- Social media reach or influence (rate of followers, rate of engagement)
- Publishing metrics (if you're a blogger or writer)
- Website traffic
- Website conversions (how many people signed up for your newsletter, for example)

You might derive some satisfaction from tracking non-business things, too. Keep track of your fitness, sleep quality, social connections, and your personal budget.

COMMUNICATION

Have you heard that verbal communication conveys only 7% of the meaning of a message? This alarmed me when I heard it during a master class on communication. The instructor explained that the balance is 55% body language and 38% tone of voice. As a remote worker, 55% of meaning would be lost in a phone call and 93% would be lost in an email exchange!

I searched for the source of this statistic. It's based on research from UCLA Professor Albert Mehrabian's study on human communication patterns. He and his colleagues studied a very specific situation. Subjects used single words related to their feelings or attitudes. They simultaneously used non-verbal actions incongruent with the word. There are plenty of articles that aim to discount this research when it's applied to communication in general*. Whether you're recording a podcast or conducting a WebEx, your percentages are sure to be different. Body language and tone of delivery are important, but words matter far more than 7% to the listener.

Remote workers must be good writers. After all, most of our interactions are virtual! Written communication is prevalent, persistent, and therefore important. How many of these do you interact with daily? Emails, instant messaging, business requirements, Slack updates, wiki pages, trouble tickets, and texting threads. We've all been on the receiving end of bad communication. Poorly organized thoughts can be amplified by the wrong words.

People will judge you based on the quality of your communication. Communication can seal the deal or hold you back. It's your choice.

Step 1: Organize your thoughts

Optimize the structure of your message. If you're summarizing something complex, think about the data and logic you used. Structure your writing to influence the reader. It's easy to spot this kind of writing — it follows a logical path from start to finish.

Step 2: Use the right words

Consider your audience. If you're an academic writing about a niche topic to outsiders, you have to adjust how you're communicating. I'm a technologist and know that my writing is technical and direct if I'm writing to peers. When I communicate to my manager, I avoid using too much jargon. Use words sparingly. If you can say it in five words, why use ten? I write everything down first to get it out of my brain. Then I edit ruthlessly, cutting 30-40% of the words to optimize reading.

Step 3: Say them the best way possible

Steps 1 and 2 are all you get when you're writing. When you're giving a speech or leading a meeting (in-person or remote), Step 3 can be the icing on your communication cake. One of the best things my parents did for me was to get me lessons from a public speaking coach. I won an award and I had to give a speech. The coach's advice still resonates with me:

- **Speak more slowly than you think you should.**
  I'm a fast talker, so this one was difficult! It'll seem unnatural to you when you slow down. It doesn't play that way to the audience, though.

- **Vary your tone and cadence to match what you're saying.**
  Nobody likes a monotone delivery. It's boring. Be dynamic!

- **Make eye contact with your audience.**
  Eye contact engages listeners. I look ahead in my notes for what's coming, then look up and deliver the next few sentences. I rarely look directly at people. I look at an imaginary wall in front of them or just above their heads. They can't tell the difference!

- **If you can, move.**
  I love it when people talking on stage walk and use body language to help express their words. It can be frustrating to listen to a person behind a lectern for long stretches of time. Some of my best phone calls are when I'm walking around the room, headset on, being a full participant in the call.

- **Smile!**
  It's contagious.

I apply these lessons anytime I'm speaking: one-on-one with a friend or colleague, during a conference call, or behind a lectern on a stage. I recommend taking public speaking courses. Lynda.com, an online learning library, has several public speaking courses. Of course, practice is the best education, so take every opportunity to stand up and make your voice heard!

** https://www.psychologytoday.com/blog/beyond-words/201109/
is-nonverbal-communication-numbers-game,
http://www.virtualspeechcoach.com/2014/05/07/is-
communication-really-93-non-verbal*

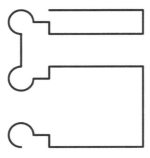

Task Management

There are plentiful techniques and tools for managing tasks. The most important thing you can do is to pick one and stick with it. Don't waste time looking for a more perfect tool! Find one that works for you and start using it. You're unique and have your own workflow. Once you find something that meets your requirements, start using it. You can always adjust later if it's not working for you.

I have been using Todoist to track tasks. I use Apple Notes to keep more extensive notes about those tasks or save information for later. Todoist lets you set due dates and reminders, too. I don't have to keep tasks and dates in my brain — I've relegated them all to the systems in my life. I love being reminded when something is due! I segment my task lists like this:

- **To Do:** short-term tasks to do today or within weeks

- **Waiting on Others:** tasks waiting on another step before I can pick them up again

- **Development Ideas:** longer-term tasks and ideas for future work. When I start work on one, it may become multiple short-term tasks in "To Do"

- **Movies to Watch:** this is a great way to record things to watch. When someone mentions a movie or show they've seen that sounds interesting, I put it here.

- **To Buy:** things that are "nice to have" that I'd like to purchase. Not now. But soon. A "better pizza cutter" has been on there for awhile so I should probably get rolling on that.

I also use IFTTT as a reminder service. You can choose from tons of data-driven applets. I started using it to repost my Instagrams as native photos on Facebook and Twitter. My favorite applet type is calendar-based, triggering email notifications to me:

- Daily, to use a tool for Twitter audience management

- Monthly, to schedule acupuncture (odd months) or massage (even months). I really look forward to getting this reminder!

- Monthly, to get in touch with people I want to maintain relationships with. This one is super important to me. It reminds me to reach out and schedule something — anything. People get busy, and if too much time goes by, relationships can languish.

I also love IFTTT's RSS alert. When anything is added to an RSS feed I get an email. For example, if a new job is added to an online job board or when a friend adds a new blog post. I don't have to use a fancy feed reader and I don't have to remember to go to someone's website to check for something new. Technology does its best work when it saves me time!

My tools and techniques for managing tasks and information flow change over time. But, the concept of "Inbox Zero" has been with me since I started working after college. I know there are many approaches to email management and they all have their places. I can't stand having a vertical scroll bar in my email program, though. I see my inbox as a short task list. If I have more than a screenful of messages, that's a problem. Here's how I get to Inbox Zero:

- If an email doesn't require a response and doesn't need to be saved, I delete it.

- If it doesn't require a response but might come in handy later, I archive it in a subject-based folder.

- If it requires a response and can be done quickly, I respond in the moment and archive the message.

- If it requires a longer response or will take more time than I have, I flag it and come back to it later.

I feel a great sense of accomplishment on the few occasions that I've been able to achieve Inbox Zero. There's one truism, though — the emails will keep coming!

MANAGING REMOTE TEAMS

Management techniques can be applied in three directions: to yourself, up, and down. Much of this book is dedicated to managing yourself as a remote worker, helping set you up for success. This chapter focuses on what you might term traditional management: managing down. I managed a team of designers and developers in the United States and India between 2006 and 2013.

Sure, it was less expensive to have part of my team in another country, but the key benefit I saw was productivity gains. We were able to support other regions during their normal business hours. Support and development tasks followed the sun. They started in one time zone and finished in another. We also had good coverage during country-specific holidays.

It was a unique situation: I was remote and most of my team was in a traditional office. It's tough to gauge how the team is doing when you're not there in person. You miss out on casual interactions, lunches, and after-work drinks. It can be difficult to find common meeting times across time zones. Days of productivity can be lost due to misunderstandings or late feedback.

Remote management thrives on communication, collaboration, creative scheduling, and mutual respect. As a manager, be supportive, direct, honest, knowledgeable and trustworthy.

Build Rapport

You have to rely on voice, email and chat since you're seldom face-to-face with your team. If possible, meet your team in person and establish some rapport. It'll ease future interactions if you understand each person's background and personality. Professional encounters are more effective when you have more insight into the person. Jackson, one of my former teammates, said it best:

> *"Personal rapport is critical, and for all the books, tutorials, speaking tours and management consultancies promoting teamwork, I don't recall this even being mentioned. Yet it's how we build human relationships, which is the natural basis of loyalty and teamwork. It's just common sense: a group of people who like each other, who understand each other and have a personal relationship will want to stick together and help each other out to get a problem solved. Feeling this affinity with a manager makes the team so much stronger and, I'm assuming, prevents a blame culture from blossoming."*

We're not all comedians, but humor can go a long way in establishing rapport. Have fun with each other. Laughing about a shared experience, especially work-related, is a great way to strengthen a relationship.

Meet as a Group

We met daily to review designs, talk about what happened the prior day, and discuss roadblocks. I strived to keep the daily meeting efficient and brief. I had people share updates in a random order — a decision that turned out to be particularly effective. With a predictable order, people tune out unless it's their turn to talk. The randomness kept them on their toes. One of my teammates told me that they enjoyed this aspect of team meetings.

Jackson observed that when you have a mix of on-site and remote participants, it can create a dichotomy of "people in the room" vs. "people on the phone." There's a sense of equality if everyone is dialed in and collaborating virtually. I've definitely seen this before, when the "people in the room" seem to take priority over those on the phone. In 100% virtual meetings, even with the same group of participants, it's more of a level playing field. At my current company, participants in smaller meetings are 100% virtual, whereas our daily status meeting has about ⅓ of the participants in the room. We've had the meeting for so long, though, that no such dichotomy is evident.

Meet One-on-One

I met one-on-one with my direct reports at least once a week. As a result, I knew what anyone was working on at any time, and also got to know them better as people. It's not micromanagement, mind you, but a specific awareness of what's "in flight" with the team. I was better prepared to give updates to my own managers when I focused on understanding my team's work.

Conduct the Orchestra

Management is like conducting an orchestra. As the conductor, you should know the music and the players inside and out. You should be able to point to a section (oboes, trumpets, percussion) and know what they're supposed to be doing. However, when a composition could be better, conductors don't abandon their perch. You don't see them rush into a section and start playing along (or worse, replacing a musician). Don't micromanage. Trust your team to do the right thing and give them the tools to do it. Trust, but verify. Yes, it's your responsibility to know what's going on. It's not your responsibility to micromanage, taking creative license and ownership away. Lastly, don't have meetings because you think you should. Meetings are for collaboration, not "telling people things." Continuing the orchestra analogy, you don't assemble the orchestra and not have them play. If you're telling them something, send them an email instead.

Clear Roadblocks
I made sure my team knew that part of my job was to clear roadblocks, that they could come to me with any problem. I never wanted to learn about something after the opportunity to correct it had passed. I gave my own managers the same courtesy. If there was a problem I couldn't handle on my own, I involved them early to help clear roadblocks.

Give Credit
Managers are less likely to be an individual contributors. Most of the work that you promote is not your own: it was done by your team. Give your people the opportunity to shine. Have them present their work in meetings where senior managers are present. Don't take credit for their work! You may be the manager, and may have helped create the climate for your team to work, but they actually did it. Didn't people lift you up and

give you opportunities to be visible earlier in your career? It's time to pay it forward.

Give Feedback

Give your team constructive feedback. Feedback can build people up and make them stronger. People are your greatest asset. Your honest feedback should aim to help your people grow, not cut them down. Give feedback regularly, not just at annual review time. We've all been there: no feedback is no picnic.

Be Available

Who's had a manager with an "open door" policy? My experience varies, but some managers with this policy are so busy they're rarely available. Their email overflows and they don't respond to instant messages or voicemails. Don't be that person. Be available for your team.

As a remote manager there's no visual cue for your team to know if you're available. Institute a culture where they know if they call you, email you or start a chat with you, you're there and responsive. Jackson shared with me:

> *"It was always easy to contact you, I never felt that you were trying to "hide" as it were."*

Be friendly and approachable. Your team should feel free to share opinions without fearing consequences. They should share personal details and discover, with delight, that they're not alone. They can realize that their manager has fears, hopes and dreams ... like they do.

Be Accountable

Don't throw your team under the bus. The buck stops with you. I've seen plenty of managers deflect criticism of something their team did. There are always mitigating circumstances, but examine the factors you control. When reflecting on something that didn't go as planned, think about what role you played. What could you have done to create a different outcome? Sure, your team will make mistakes. Sure, there are external factors. You as a manager, though, have some level of control. You might identify several things that you influenced (or could have) and learn from them.

Stick to the Plan

Be organized. Be visionary. Play the long game. Reactionary bosses cultivate stressful environments. Things go more smoothly if you have a well-publicized plan. If you're doing some of the following things, you'll end up leading a team with poor morale:

- Ignoring or constantly shifting deadlines
- Having urgent unplanned meetings to resolve issues
- Tolerating last-minute changes without a strong governance process

Have the Tough Conversations

Even if you're doing all the right things, management isn't all sunshine and roses. People will have issues that have little bearing on their actual work. That's why it is important to manage the person, not the work. I never felt like an employee duped me: when there was a family emergency or medical issue, it was legitimate. When employees are disengaged or disenfranchised, they won't operate at their best. If someone has a personal issue that affects their work, see if they'll open up to you. There may be a way to help. Engage HR, offer a benefit like flex time, or talk through the issue as if you were speaking with a friend. Yet, there are times when rapport and communication will fail you. I had an employee who was taking advantage of the team. This employee wasn't a team player, missed deadlines, and griped about everything. Take action if you have a toxic presence on your team. Teams can be held back when a manager allows someone to underperform. Inaction is also a choice! Address issues head on within the guidelines your Human Resources team gives you. We tried to mentor the employee through performance reviews, provided informal feedback, and took careful notes about interactions that could have been improved. When we were tasked with trimming our department a short time later, the employee had not improved. Our choice was easier because of our active engagement and documentation.

Get to know the people on your team beyond a purely professional level. What motivates them? What are their concerns? Knowing the whole person will help you more effectively lead them.

If you lead team meetings, have people share their updates in a random order. It'll keep them on their toes and keep things lively. They'll be less likely to tune out, too.

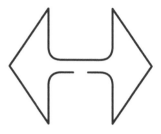

Managing Up

It's tempting to think that management is not in your list of job responsibilities if nobody reports to you. Regardless of your role, it's critical that you "manage up" to your managers.

It's tough to be visible when you're remote. You have to be a passionate advocate for yourself. It's the only way to counter the "out of sight, out of mind" realities that remote work reinforces.

Make your contributions heard. I summarize my weekly accomplishments for my technology, business and QA partners. They're aware of what I'm working on and can ask questions about things that may impact them. If I've done something for someone outside my group, I share that with my team and manager, too. Bonus points if you get a thank you note from another group or a client. I forward those messages to my manager and file them away in a "Kudos" folder for annual review time.

Advocate for your professional advancement. Strive to grow and learn, regardless of your tenure. These opportunities are rarely given to you — you have to seek them out! I've rarely been denied after asking for professional development opportunities. Employers are happy to learn that employees are thirsty for more knowledge. They'll have a more satisfied employee and you'll gain new skills you can apply on the job.

Opportunities abound with online learning libraries, professional development, conferences, and seminars. Look around and see what you're interested in!

Ask to be involved. If you'd like to work on a new project, ask how you can help. If you hear about a meeting that you think you should be at, your exclusion might be an oversight. Ask to be included and then contribute to the conversation once you're there. After you have several of these interactions, you'll need to be less proactive to be included.

Make the most of travel. For some people, travel presents more of an opportunity for networking than it does work. Try to meet senior managers and other colleagues you don't normally interact with. When you're remote you don't get to have random encounters with people in the hallway or kitchenette. Make the most of your physical time together and it'll pay dividends when you're back in your remote office.

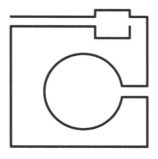

DISCIPLINE

One of the common responses when I tell people I work remotely is, "Oh, I don't know how you have the discipline for that!" I respond with a wry smile because it IS difficult. Discipline takes discipline. Certain people may have more natural discipline, but it is a skill you can improve.

Expectations are set in an office environment. You know after what arrival time your manager will raise her eyebrows. You know before what departure time your boss will pull you aside and say, "Exactly where is it you have to be?" The people around you keep you on task and in your seat, unless you're in a meeting, on your way to or from one.

All bets are off when you're remote. You can start when you want. Finish when you want. Go for a walk when you want. Your manager and peers won't notice, and that's okay! In the grand scheme of things, it doesn't matter. What matters is that you get your job done. Discipline is the way that'll happen without anyone raising their eyebrows.

You're in charge of your work day. Stick to reliable start and end times and respect those boundaries. I never check work email before work, and after work only if there's an ongoing support issue I'm involved in. Reliable start and end times also help your family and friends plan around your schedule. Remember when I wrote about my experience working in Switzerland? The Swiss arrived and left punctually, and I learned quite a lesson when I worked late and found myself alone, locked in the darkened office building. Looking back on the years my children were growing up, my punctuality was a critical part of my work/life balance. They knew that when I was working, I couldn't be with the family. They also knew that when I said I'd be done, I was done and fully involved in meals, games, and hanging out. In that sense, my job was rather transparent to the rest of the family, even though I was was always just a few steps away.

Enjoy that midday break called lunch. Block off a full midday hour in your work calendar so that time is not taken by last-minute meetings. Take time to smell the roses, whatever they may be for you. Sure, there will be days where you have to shorten your lunch, or days when you meet a friend for a longer lunch. Schedule that time for yourself and safeguard it to the extent possible.

You can choose how to structure your day most effectively. If you focus better in the morning, do work that requires focus then. You might prefer the afternoon when you tune out the world and drive toward quitting time. Whenever those times of day are for you, screen out distractions and be productive.

Chores are Distracting

Distractions are guaranteed, though. That's what my friends mean when they say they wouldn't have the discipline to work remotely. Laundry. Dishes. Floors. Cleaning. Groceries. The list goes on! If you're not careful, every day could look like a cleaning day. It helps to have a dedicated space where you can be away from visual reminders of other things that need to get done. Processes can help, too. I have a 2-week rotation of "things that need doing" that I keep in a list. When a chore's day comes up, I do it and then stop. Each chore has its day and I'm not tempted to rush ahead. If I do one of these during a break in my day, or before it begins, I feel accomplished and can re-focus my efforts on working. Here's what that rotation looks like:

	Even Weeks	Odd Weeks
Monday	Clean Office	Garage
Tuesday	Stove	Kitchen Floor
Wednesday	Vacuum Upstairs	Dust
Thursday	Vacuum Downstairs	Organize Pantry
Friday	Bathrooms	Wash Bedding

Apps are Distracting, Too

I had a gaming problem earlier in my career. If I was bored or between tasks, I would fire up Need for Speed or Age of Empires. I had a steering wheel accessory for the driving game, and a round of Age of Empires could take hours. I moved virtual armies and trebuchets around when I should have been more productive. The quickest (and most effective) way to get rid of a bad habit like this is to lose the game. I uninstalled and sold them both. In the long run, I didn't miss them.

The proliferation of apps on our devices has the potential to introduce the same problem. There are games that take a few minutes, which is fine. There are games that can consume hours, and those are not fine. In fact, they may have been designed to prey on addictive tendencies. I recognize those for what they are, delete them, and am far happier (and productive) for it. Your productivity nemesis may be games, chores, or something else. Be vigilant: recognize anything that is taking up far too much of your time and kick it to the curb.

Reward and Enrich Yourself

Discipline isn't just about avoiding things that suck productivity from your day. It's also about ensuring you do the things that enrich your life and bring you joy! I wish I had focused on this earlier in my career. I recently started focusing more on wellness and reinforcing positive habits. Take fitness, for example. I've chosen an annual challenge (and some years, more than one) with my wife since 2006. We rode around Cayuga Lake on our mountain bikes that year. Boy, that was painful. We purchased road bikes soon after!

We ran our first half marathon together in 2007. We've been choosing challenges since then: triathlons, road running, and trail running. They all need proper planning and training. The actual goal is like a victory lap — the real reward of an ambitious goal is the training leading up to it. A training plan is a wonderful thing. Discipline is inherent in the plan. You can't "cram" for a race. Put in the daily work and you will reap the long-term rewards.

I run in the morning or around lunchtime. It's one of the key benefits of working remotely! I can get out my front door for a workout without much forethought. If my run is lasts an hour, I'm gone from my desk for an hour.

I incorporate smaller goals in my day, too. Some become habits and some are experiments. Streaks is a great app for iOS devices (similar apps exist for other devices, too). I use it to record activities that I'd like to turn into habits. It's satisfying to check things off and see how many continuous days you've been doing it! I've had streaks for:

- **Drawing:** I drew daily in 2016 and called it my #365DayDraw. I posted a scan of the drawing each day on Twitter along with a witty comment. This was my most fulfilling streak!

- **Push-ups:** I do push-ups every morning while my coffee is heating up. I started doing 25 per day, but that got easier over time. I thought, "Why not do my age in push-ups, so when I have a birthday I'll have to add one?" I've been doing this for 1,193 days straight as I write this.

- **Writing:** I write for a half hour each weekday morning before 6 am. It's great to make progress on writing projects or blog posts, and a half hour is a great amount of time. I wrote this book during this daily writing time.

- **Language:** I took French in high school, and thought it'd be fun to pick up some Spanish, too. My kids liked using Duolingo in school, so I installed it on my phone and got started. It just take a few minutes each day. *Realmente.*

- **Lynda.com:** I have an annual subscription to Lynda.com's online learning library. I'm learning a new programming language at the moment (Ruby on Rails). I have taken a lot of their programming and illustration courses, too.

- **Music:** I started playing guitar as an adult and have a goal to practice for a half hour every weekday.

- **Crossword:** The New York Times has a great app for crossword puzzles. They release a free mini puzzle each day. It takes just a few minutes but it's a fun brain exercise. My wife and I race to see who can solve it first.

- **Bible:** The app from bible.com is great for doing a plan. I have done a whole bible plan over the course of a year, and smaller, more inspirational plans. You can configure it to email you each day so you have another reminder.

Block out an hour for lunch on your work calendar. Make an appointment with yourself and keep it!

Ditch the negative addictions in your life. Whether they're vices or video games, you'll be happier when they're gone.

Reinforce the positive things you want to turn into habits. Use an app to give you extra motivation to get them done.

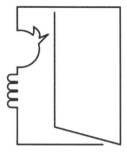

INQUISITIVENESS

I attended a huge global technology meeting during my first month on the job. I'd been in the trenches since my first day coming up to speed on the technology our group created. Employee orientations weren't a thing yet, though. I didn't have a big picture view of how the technology fit into the company's broader mission. The global meeting illustrated the breadth of the larger group I was a part of. Colleagues traveled from all over the world and we collaborated in one large room.

I wrote about how the meeting was a "defining experience" for my young mind. Here's an excerpt from my contribution to an early performance review.

> *This showed me firsthand the breadth and depth that a large corporation's technology function can face. It made me realize how much of an impact one decision could make in such a large organization. It also motivated me to learn as much as I could about the history and direction of technology in the bank to better understand those decisions.*

This philosophy would follow me for the rest of my career as a user experience professional. I interview users to learn about their experience using a product or service. I've had users lament that they cannot share more, or that their experience is not very exciting. I tell them not to worry — all data is good data, as long as it helps color in the picture you're working on. It's important to understand as much of the story as you can. Being informed helps you make better decisions.

My kids sometimes struggle with asking questions, as did I when I was their age. I thought that by asking a question, I'd be tipping my hand that I wasn't as smart as I hoped the other person thought I was. It's exactly the opposite. By asking a question, you communicate to the other person that you're engaged and interested. You signal that you want to understand something but need their help to do so.

Tim Ferriss features Ricardo Semler in one of his podcasts. Ricardo, CEO of Semco Partners in Brazil, is known for radical management approaches. Ricardo gave a TED talk on the topic in January 2017, too. He talks about how the "three whys" are a path to greater understanding. Three questions, asked in a row, break down our reflexive answers and lead to insight. They can be asked about anything.

- Ask "why?" You'll get an immediate and typically reflexive answer.

- Probe a little deeper with a follow-up "why" question. This is more difficult for the person to answer. They need to think about it.

- Go even further with another "why" question. This time, the person may realize that there's a deeper question in the questioning. It's at this point that you start to uncover true wisdom.

You can apply this to all kinds of questions that affect your happiness. Asking "why" the third time may yield a different answer than the first.

Why can't you go for a midday hike?

Why do you have to be at work each day at 8:30 a.m.?
Why do you need to check your work email during the weekend?

Why are you living in your current town or city?

Is this daily meeting necessary?

Why do we have to dress up for work?

Why do I say "yes" to every request to be involved with things?

Ask a "why" question. Then ask two more.

Being informed and honest helps you make better decisions.

Transparency

Think about an office environment you're familiar with. Now think about a particular person in that office environment. Is it a colleague or your boss? If you pay attention, you can get a good sense of where they are and what they're doing at any given time during the day. You catch a glimpse of them through the glass walls of a conference room. You hear their voice from a nearby speakerphone. You see them coming and going from the elevator banks, and you know who was walking out with them for a late lunch. There's a lot that you can learn about someone when you see them.

People don't have that when you're remote. Without communication, your team won't have much visibility into your schedule. Lack of transparency is one reason managers aren't comfortable with remote work. How will they know what you're working on — and if you're being productive — if they can't see you? The paradox is that in an office, though you may be glued to your chair, they don't know what you're doing in that chair. You could be working on something productive. Or, you could be filling in a grocery list or optimizing your fantasy football brackets. It's hard to know for sure! Was that conversation with your nearby colleague about the new TPS reports? Or, were you talking about how they discovered the fantastic new food cart on 57th and Madison? As a remote worker, find ways to be transparent. Find ways to remove shreds of doubt about your productivity.

Transparency is so easy with social media, instant messaging, texting, and video conferencing. Collaboration tools were in their infancy when I started working remotely. I had to be creative about being transparent.

We had many offices around the world and phone calls were a popular way of communicating. If someone called me and I didn't answer, it could be for a variety of reasons. I could be busy, on another call, or not there. The caller had no idea if I was preparing a cup of coffee or was in the midst of a 2-week vacation. The solution was simple: I updated my voicemail greeting daily. When I shared this tip with someone, they were bewildered. "Doesn't that take forever to do?" It's not that hard. I changed first thing every morning and the system keystrokes became muscle memory.

"Good morning, you've reached Scott Dawson. It's Friday, January 20th and I'm in the office today. Please leave a message and I'll get back to you."

Or, "I'm NOT in the office today, but I'll be back on Monday."

The beauty of this technique is that callers know if they should wait for you to get back to them or try somewhere else.

Always turn on your email auto-reply when you're going to be out of the office. It may be a day, a week, or more, but it's a great way to let people know that you're away. Include information about how they can get in touch with you or your designated backup.

If you use a calendar for group scheduling, make sure all your appointments are there. This helps others see when you are busy when scheduling a meeting. Have a haircut or a doctor's appointment? Put it in there so nobody puts a conflicting meeting in the same spot. I also block off lunch for myself each day. I used to have meetings that would encroach on or conflict with a midday lunch break. That rarely happens now that I've blocked off a midday hour.

Collaboration tools are a great way to touch base with people as if they were in the office. Instant messaging is great for quick questions. I've had geography come up in conversations with people after working with them for years. They had no idea I worked remotely. They thought I worked in another building in New York City. That's how I knew I'd nailed communication, when my colleagues assumed I worked in a different office.

There's a risk in having too much transparency when you're remote. One of my colleagues would send the team an email for the simplest things, like "headed to the auto parts store." I take breaks throughout the day, and when I do, I don't feel compelled to share. I go out for a run or grab coffee with a friend without feeling regret. Of course, I made sure I'm not shirking any scheduled responsibilities. I have my phone in case someone needs me, but we're all "big kids" now. If we can't trust each other to get our jobs done, then we shouldn't have the jobs in the first place. We should feel free to do the things we want to without feeling like we need to broadcast it to the world.

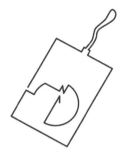

SETTING A COURSE

Imagine you're the captain at the helm of a large ship. Where are you heading? How long will it take to get there? Along the way, you'll encounter all kinds of threats and opportunities. It may be foul weather or fabulous ports of call you hadn't anticipated when you planned your journey. The joy of the situation is that you're the captain. It's up to you how you handle the trials and tribulations you'll encounter along the way.

I knew what I wanted when I started working remotely. I wanted to live outside of a major city and avoid the pressures of a daily commute. As my family grew, my motivations changed. I started placing a high value on the flexibility afforded by working remotely. I was able to have lunch with my wife and greet my kids when they got home from school. I ferried my daughter to golf practice and my son to piano practice. I did these things without sacrificing productivity. Flexibility is a priceless perk of remote work.

I'm nearing the end of my kids-living-at-home phase of life and I've never second-guessed the decision I made. That's not to say there haven't been temptations along the way to deviate from the course I set. There were genuine brushes with increased financial wealth and opportunity. At the same time, wealth isn't derived only from the size of your bank account. My emotional bank account is rather full.

I did some web design work for a startup in 1998. A college friend co-founded it. I know I could have engineered more involvement in this early-stage company. It would have been a total commitment, full days and full nights of work. I was newly married and enjoying the beginning of that journey. I played it conservatively and stuck with my modest level of nights-and-weekend consulting. A bigger company acquired them late the following year for $100 million. Was it a missed opportunity? I don't see it that way in my rear view mirror (though the money was quite nice and life-changing for those founders). True, I feel a certain regret and some bitterness about "what could have been," but the road I stayed on has been quite nice! I also shared earlier about my opportunity to join a startup in California when I was looking to transition to another job. Things were looking really good when the founders were set to embrace remote work. Negotiations fell apart, however, when their board wanted me onsite in San Jose. I passed. I didn't want the stress of flying cross-country for years to see my family on weekends. I also wouldn't have been happy working at a place where people were inherently doubtful of my value unless I was physically there. That startup was acquired several years later for an undisclosed sum. Another missed opportunity? Perhaps. But perhaps not. I'm living a modest middle-class suburban life and my kids are well-adjusted and happy. I wouldn't have it any other way.

My wife and I have been on this journey together and our plan has several milestones. The first one was building our house. We planned for it, saved for it, and accomplished it. We're planning retirement (semi-retirement?) if we can make it work. We love Oregon, so during the housing crisis several years ago we bought a townhouse there. We rent it out and will live there when we travel in the future. When we're quasi-retired, we may live a bi-coastal life. We'll have one foot in Oregon and the other in New York, depending on the time of year. It's exciting!

Don't be complacent with the status quo. There's the adage "if you fail to plan, you plan to fail." The point I'm making is not quite so dire but it is important to have a goal and chart a course toward it. Without a goal the days will drift by. Don't look up one day and ask, "Where did all the time go?"

What's your goal? Once you know, set a course and be happy with it. It's up to you whether you course-correct, 'cause that's life. Make no mistake: you're in charge. You're the captain.

EVOLUTION

Things will always change, regardless of your industry. I found out very early in my career that things never remain constant. Managers come and go. Policies change. Companies buy and integrate other companies. Technologies rise and fall in popularity. Change is inevitable! The important part is how you react to it. Some changes are unsavory, and you might rail against them and rally the troops. You must simply embrace other changes the best you can.

Remember earlier where I gave this tip?

> *"Whether encountering a new country, a new culture or a new person, know your audience. Do your research. Ask questions. It'll help tailor your interaction for success."*

That totally applies when "change" darkens your door.

I've worked for 18 different managers over 22 years in corporate life. Some were around for years. Some came in the dark of night, made some rapid unsavory changes and were gone again in a jiffy. If you've seen the Dilbert cartoon about the bungee boss, it's an apt depiction.

When I meet a new colleague or manager, I remember first that they're a person. After all, it's a biological imperative until we have cyborgs on the job! We all have hopes, dreams, fears and insecurities like the next person. I like to discover who they are, what their history is, and what they hope to do. This increases the chance of a positive and fruitful relationship, even if measured in months, not years. I had several relationships sour only to be saved by communication. Talking goes a long way towards solving most issues, or reducing the chance they'll see the light of day. If you're particularly concerned about making a good impression with someone new, do your research. Ask others who may know what they're like, what agendas they might have coming into the role, and what things you might need to watch out for. Do some basic Internet research. Where did they go to school? Where have they worked in the past, and for how long? What are their interests? All of this information can be useful in helping you get to know each other.

The mix of people around you will always be fluid. But what about when the environment changes: the premises, the policies, the technology? Chances are there's a few incremental things you can (and should) do in your job:

- If something has changed for the worse, remember "this, too, shall pass"

- Keep pace with your industry's changes in technology

- Be aware of industry trends

The Internet industry changed at a staggering rate over the 22+ years I've worked in it. I did not hunker down inside the walls of my company and ignore what was happening, though. I saw the importance of keeping an ear on what was happening in the industry and evolving along with it. I'm at an inflection point in my job where we're considering migrating to a new technology. I'm so comfortable with what we use now, the thought of "starting over" with something new makes my stomach hurt. At the end of the day, though, I know intellectually that it'll be fine. After all, it's a technology that's risen in popularity and used at a lot of companies. Not bad to put on a resume, right? We can all learn new tricks. This is just another one in the long line of tricks I've learned. Let's do it!

Here are some ideas for keeping up with what's going on in your industry. The list has a technical bent but you can adapt it for your specialty:

- **Higher Education Learning Libraries:** Many colleges and universities offer courses online. I learned how to program my first iPhone app by taking CS 193P at Stanford University for free. You can find a lot of these courses in the iTunes U library. You can find online curriculum at Michigan, Toronto, Princeton, Berkeley and more.

- **Commercial Learning Libraries:** I subscribe to Lynda.com and there are myriad others like Treehouse and Codecademy. Lynda.com is great for programming languages, software, and getting creative insight.

- **Twitter:** I joined Twitter when I was looking for a new job. I followed thought leaders in my field, especially those focusing on web design, HTML and CSS. You can do the same — find people who are doing work that you already do, or want to do. Read what they publish and you'll get a good sense of industry trends. You can also share your own material and establish a reputation.

- **Podcasts:** There are likely many podcasts in your industry. Like Twitter, these are great for getting information first-hand from industry thought leaders. I used them to get a good sense of where I should focus my professional development efforts. If you have a commute, this is a fantastic way to pass the time. I don't have a commute, so I listen to podcasts when I go on long weekend runs.

- **Industry Publications:** You can still subscribe to a lot of printed material, but online is far easier. Subscribe to the RSS feeds and email lists of your favorite publishers. You'll never want for something to read! I subscribe to Fast Company's Design newsletter and Smashing Magazine. Texture offers a paid subscription for current and back editions of many traditional magazines. Check your local library, too. They may offer free digital magazine subscriptions as part of your membership.

- **Conferences and Meetups:** Can you attend an industry conference? You may need to travel but it's worth it to hear directly from speakers and mingle with like-minded guests. If you cannot attend, some conferences post some of their material online. Try a Meetup, too: they're smaller local gatherings of people focused on a specific topic. They're also a great way to meet people, build your network, and reinforce your industry knowledge.

- **Independent Projects:** Do you want to learn a new language or have an idea for a new website? Build it yourself. My personal projects have not made me wealthy but they've all taught me something. I've done small projects that last a day and larger ones that span months.

With some of the resources above, you'll have the skills to learn something new along the way, too.

One of the best decisions I ever made was to focus on being a lifelong learner. Coupled with nights-and-weekends freelancing, this keeps my skills sharp and current. I never learned a new skill that I wasn't able to apply in another freelancing project or at my day job. It became a thing: as I was learning something new, I knew in the back of my mind that it would come in handy somehow. I didn't know the specifics at the time, but I knew from experience that it would.

Continuous learning also positioned me to interview well for a new job when the time came. I was not oblivious to the change that happened around me. Freelancing and independent learning helped me keep up with new technologies.

Having a rock solid foundation is also helpful. With programming languages, for example, it's critical to have a solid foundation. There are common algorithms and patterns that underpin most, if not all, languages. Learning a tool or a language is great, but it'll be difficult if you lack a solid foundation. If you're a programmer, the concepts of abstraction, iteration, recursion, and data structures apply to most languages. If you can wrap your mind around concepts before you work on tools and languages, you'll be far better off.

That's what employers want to see, by the way. Tools are important, yes! You don't see jobs for rock-solid recursion specialists, but you do for rock-star Ruby developers. You'll be ahead of the pack if you can prove you're a quick study. Can you think on your feet? Do you know how to use your resources to solve problems? Can you learn on the job? That will set you apart.

I was inspired to learn about Ruby on Rails by a podcast. I thought it'd be a perfect way to showcase my #365DayDraw project. I took a Lynda.com course but it required more work on the server than I wanted. I decided to roll up my sleeves and use the latest version of Angular for the same project. You can see the result at 365daydraw.scottpdawson.com. That's how you continuously learn: identify an opportunity, research, execute. Lather. Rinse. Repeat.

Continuous learning played a crucial role in my mid-career job transition. The company couldn't afford a full-time designer. They needed someone with the technical skills to code in JavaScript, too. Despite coding not being part of my prior day job, lifelong learning helped me compete and win against other qualified candidates. It can work for you, too!

COMBATING LONELINESS

Loneliness is cited as one of the main drawbacks of working remotely (along with first cousins "isolation" and "depression") so I think it's appropriate to share here. I have had periods where I've definitely felt lonely, even depressed. Changing workplaces are a major impetus for this emotion but I think it runs deeper. I think three societal changes have created a breeding ground where loneliness can thrive.

1. The death of the proverbial front porch.

In my community, and I suspect many others, the literal front porch has shrunk in size or been fully eliminated from homes. The front porch as a metaphor is not lost on me. Nobody sits "out front" anymore, exposed to whoever happens by. Interactions are superficial. Rarely are you invited to someone's backyard where secrets are bestowed, emotions shared, insecurities laid bare.

2. Loose connections and the rise of social media.

How many followers do you have? What was your engagement this week? Did the people you wanted to like your post even see your post? We're all about the metrics, constantly scrolling and refreshing to see what's new. Beyond the like and retweets, the deeper level of engagement is a comment or reply, and rarely does that get beyond what you'd say to someone in passing. Conversations in real life, even when superficial, are far more engaging.

3. Selfishness.

This word has so many negative connotations, and I don't mean them all in this context. When given a choice, and probably due to a combination of the above two phenomena, we focus on serving ourselves rather than serving the general community. When we're all promoters of ourselves, the sounds of the social media echo chambers can be deafening. There needs to be more of helping your neighbor; supporting a cause you believe in; doing something because it's the right thing to do, not because of how your status will be elevated because of it.

Okay, enough of that. *Let's get back to the loneliness and depression!*

During one of my recent troughs of emotional turmoil (and there are peaks and troughs, for sure), I paraphrased how I was feeling for my acupuncturist. I told her that one day I was fine and another was massively emotional again. I hopefully asked, "Is there something you can do to help reset, or re-center, me?"

She told me about the "7 Emotions" in traditional Chinese medical theory. She explained that an excess of any of these most common emotions (joy, anger, anxiety, overthinking, grief, fear and fright) could cause dis-ease in the body. That spelling is intentional: dis-ease representing a lack of feeling of ease or well-being, as well as potential illness. Rather than holding strong emotions in and allowing them to create tension and illness, my acupuncturist talked about methods for releasing them in traditional Chinese medicine:

- physical expression *(exercise, acupuncture, tai chi)*
- mental/emotional expression *(writing, talking about feelings, therapy)*

In addition, she noted more traditional methods for calming the body and mind, including acupuncture, tai chi, yoga, meditation and breathing techniques. We talked about how I already physically express things through exercise and acting, and emote using writing (see: this book), therapy, and a fledgling meditation practice. She said the treatment she'd give me would include acupuncture points that would promote the smooth movement of energy in my body and calm and settle my mind. Normally I walk out of a treatment feeling relaxed, almost foggy in the aftermath of the acupuncture. This time, I walked out with a sense of clarity and purpose I'd not felt in a long time. My acupuncturist smiled at me and said, "Nice, isn't it?" Yes, it was. I think I'll ask for that treatment again!

So, how can you overcome loneliness when you're working remotely? I don't have all the answers. If I did, I wouldn't be writing this chapter! I do think that sharing how you feel, first with yourself, is an essential first step.

I know I'm not alone, either. When I shared a poll on the @workingrem Twitter account, followed mostly by remote workers, 53% of the respondents said they were often or sometimes lonely, with another 13% saying they wouldn't share if they were. I think there's a perceived stigma to speaking up about this type of emotion.

A quick online search can reveal popular suggestions for combating loneliness. I've listed some below, along with my thoughts on how each applies to my own situation.

Take the first step and reach out to others. If at first you don't succeed, try, try again. The person may be busy now, but they might not be at another time.

I'm wired to think that someone is rejecting me when they say they can't get together. When you chain enough "I'm sorry, but I'm busy" responses together, how can you not think that it's not worth the effort? It is easier to just forget it and move on, but your assumption may also be incorrect. I've tried (with varying success) to have reminders to get in touch with specific people every few weeks or months. Sometimes we get so busy that time slips by. It's nice to have the reminder to check in, even if it's just a quick phone call or a cup of coffee.

Set a goal to meet someone new each month. Then, do something social with them!

This is hard for me to do reliably. I've reached out to someone new maybe twice in the last year? The idea implies that I've met enough "new" people to ask them to do something. So, just like a conversion funnel, perhaps I need to find opportunities to meet more people in order to be able to ask a percentage of them to have coffee.

It's tempting to limit conversation with close friends to your job or your family. Be honest and talk about your feelings, too! Candor breeds closer friendships.

This one is tough for me, since I don't feel like I have many close friends. It's almost like a chicken and egg problem, where being honest about your life with someone might help you achieve that closeness, and subsequently make it okay to be honest. I've focused, then, on being honest wherever I can. Sometimes it may push someone away, and other times it may bring them closer. I don't know until I try, though.

I recently read about the concept of "36 Questions" as a way of deepening ties between people. The questions come from the results of a study titled "The Experimental Generation of Interpersonal Closeness" in Personality and Social Psychology Bulletin (1997). In the study, social psychology researcher Arthur Aron argues that the questions can make two people feel better about each other and want to meet again. The questions share a common thread of vulnerability, honesty, and openness, and you might find inspiration in them for your next meeting with someone you'd like to be closer with.

Don't be alone for special occasions and holidays. You won't be lonely when it matters most to you!

I'm lucky to have family around me all the time, so this idea is easy to check off. My wife's parents and my parents are both in the same town with us, too. My wife is super supportive and we're each other's best friend. We don't place a lot of emphasis on birthdays or holidays, but we do get together with extended family for the major holidays. If you're alone, though, I can see this being critically important. The hardest part is making the plan and getting in on the calendar. Look ahead and make plans for the times when you're sure you won't want to be all alone in your home.

Feel alone sometimes at work? Do something that brings you joy during your lunch break, either by yourself or with others.

I'm nailing this one. When my wife is home during the day with me, we make a point to go for a walk after lunch. I take breaks during the day for fitness, to work on learning a new language using Duolingo, or playing the guitar.

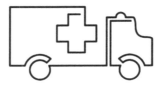

GET INVOLVED

I'm an introvert. I married one, too. We took a Myers-Briggs personality type indicator test as part of a church function. We each took our tests on our own: I was on an airplane; my wife was in our apartment. We arrived at the next church function eager to find out our results. They split the room into two halves: introverts on one side and extroverts on the other. Anyone who came into the room at that point would have known exactly what was going on. One side of the room was active, engaged, talkative, squirmy, and lively. The other side was quiet, standing in inwardly-focused postures. They shared awkward smiles with each other and waited for what was coming next. We stood on the introvert side. It was hilarious.

They continued halving the groups, resulting in 16 squares. Each square represented a permutation of the Myers-Briggs' four-letter rankings. One other person stood in my square: my wife. We were the only INFJs (introversion, intuition, feeling, judging) in the room. Breaking this down a bit:

- **More introverted than extroverted:** Quiet. Prefers a few close friends to a wider group of looser connections. Social interactions are exhausting. All true.

- **More intuitive than sensing:** More abstract than concrete. Less focused on details, more on the big picture. Long-term planning instead of focusing on what's right in front of them. Somewhat less true: I'm obsessively detail-oriented, but mostly when pursuing a big-picture goal.

- **More feeling than thinking:** Pays more attention to subjective feelings than objective observations. When deciding, logic takes a back seat to social implications. Spot on. I base decisions on my gut all the time, not on what the implications would be for me professionally or socially. I think about my feelings a lot.

- **More judging than perceiving:** Planning and making decisions are a priority, not waiting until the last minute. Desires being in control and having things turn out as predicted. Yep. We're both planners, and we don't deal well with change. Age has helped us freak out less when unforeseen things happen, but it's difficult.

How much would our INFJ status change if we took this test as adults, parents, and professionals? We were starting off as a married couple without kids when we took it the first time. Reading through the descriptions, though, I suspect ours wouldn't change much!

People who know me are shocked to find out where I fall on the introvert/extrovert spectrum. They know me as a singer, actor, and jokester. They know me as gregarious (at times), organized, and involved. It's a surprise to find out that the person that's on stage or leading a meeting is a closet introvert. It takes me a lot of energy to do these things! After doing something patently extroverted, I want to go home, pour a cup of coffee, and be alone for a while. It's like draining your electric car to the point of concern and getting it home to recharge for the evening.

That's one of the reasons I'm successful working remotely. As an introvert, I am not exhausted by being alone most of the day.

In fact, I derive energy from that. When I travel to an office I flit from meeting to meeting without breaks. At the end of the day, I hope there are no after-work activities like drinks or dinner. All I want to do is go back to the hotel, get a workout in, do some yoga, and read. This introvert is a real party animal.

I was a wreck during the opening months of my college freshman year. I didn't drink, I wasn't interested in parties, and I didn't get along with my roommate. I begged my parents to let me come home before Thanksgiving break. They gave me advice that was the antidote for my homesickness and loneliness. The advice was simple: get involved!

It made all the difference in enriching my educational experience. Being involved meant far more than going to parties and drinking the fine beer (I'm being facetious about the quality here). I got involved in more substantial ways:

- **Activities Commission:** This committee planned and executed much of the campus entertainment. I met a fantastic group of kids and adults and gained experience talking with artist agents. I was entertained by rider requirements (the amenities artists want when on tour). I personally catered to artists from the moment they stepped off their planes. I took Carrot Top (Scott Thompson) out for pizza, worked stage security for Barenaked Ladies, and was entertained by Phish and their fans.

- **Resident Advisor:** I relied on my freshman resident advisor, but less so the following year. As a sophomore I clicked very well with my roommate. I wanted to help others so I returned the favor, signing up to be an RA for my junior and senior years. The RA community was supportive and fun, and it was so fulfilling to be the go-to person for questions and care. As a bonus, I lived in a building where the RAs had single rooms my senior year. It was nice to not have a roommate, and I came to view the entire floor as my roommate. My door was open until 3 or 4 in the morning and then I slept 'til 10 or 11 the next day.

- **Alpha Phi Omega:** I learned the value of service as a Boy Scout. I was naturally interested in Alpha Phi Omega, a co-ed national service-based fraternity. It was not a traditional party-going fraternity. I pledged my junior year and enjoyed two years of "leadership, fellowship and service" with like-minded kids. I met some of my best college friends in APO.

- **Emergency Squad:** My college had a student-run emergency squad. We called the town's ambulance for true medical emergencies. We handled basic first aid and intoxication calls (our specialty) on our own. I was not a paramedic but had enough first aid and lifesaving skills to be a confident assistant. I volunteered as a driver, paired with a paramedic, for each 12-hour shift. We helped people in so many ways. The most memorable call came in on a sunny spring afternoon. We heard a radio call about a motorcycle accident on the bypass that bisects campus. The call was not our purview given the accident location on the bypass, but we were minutes away. We responded with lights flashing. The motorcyclist was in bad shape with a heavy neck laceration and likely broken bones. We were first on scene, and it was surreal. Nobody else was around, not even onlookers. We addressed the patient's most urgent issues while waiting for the ambulance to arrive. As we worked, I realized in horror that I knew the motorcyclist. He was one of my fellow computer science students. He thankfully made a full recovery.

- **Racquetball:** My Dad taught me how to play racquetball. I brought my racquet to college and discovered that one of my calculus study partners knew how to play. We played frequently and I took a 1-credit racquetball class to hone my skills. I rotated through a few partners on the court but my favorite opponent was my study partner. After all, we'd get married years later!

Being so involved in undergraduate school helped me transition to graduate school. My Masters program at Cornell lasted a year (the length of the program). Unlike my fellow graduate students, I had two social networks as soon as I arrived. First, I sought out the local Alpha Phi Omega chapter. Their ranks were full of undergraduates. They were happy (and curious) to have a graduate school member. I enjoyed fellowship and the chance to volunteer again. It was a nice respite from the engineering lab work!

Second, I signed up as a graduate community assistant, or GCA (graduate school's RA equivalent). I didn't have much time to focus on myself. My residents came first and I enjoyed helping them each day. On one of my first days at Schuyler House, a Chinese student who didn't speak much English asked me how to write a check. He had never had a checkbook before. We got through the tutorial using limited English, gestures, and symbols. Schuyler House was diverse. Its residents were aspiring lawyers, MBAs, and a few other engineers like me. My fellow GCA was an aspiring lawyer. We made strong social connections with our residents and the other GCAs on campus.

Wherever you are on the introvert/extrovert spectrum, get involved. It can help with the isolation and loneliness you might experience working remotely. When I worked in an office some of my strongest connections were with colleagues. As a remote worker, that's shifted. My strongest connections are with people I see every day, like my wife and kids. That's a good thing! People you're close to might be involved in something that you'd like, too! It may be as simple as talking about it, or making a bigger commitment and volunteering your time.

Here are some other ideas to get involved.

- Join a fire department auxiliary, or be a volunteer firefighter
- Help build a house with Habitat for Humanity
- Join a faith-based organization for fellowship and social activities
- Help with food pantry distribution
- Get involved with youth organizations
- Join a running group through a local running store
- Join Rotary or Chamber of Commerce
- Help out with civic groups that help spruce up your community
- Volunteer at local festivals or concerts
- Organize a local 5K fundraiser
- Volunteer at your local library
- Sing in a community chorus
- Go to a local meetup (see meetup.com)
- Work at a coworking space a few days a week
- Attend concerts or classes at a local college or university

If you have kids, the list of opportunities can easily get longer! We've been involved with our kids' sports, school activities, PTA/PTO, theatre, music, and scouting. I've gained some unique skills and insight as a race administrator and referee for alpine ski racing.

There are so many ways to get involved, and working remotely will give you added flexibility to do so. Get out there and have some fun!

CLOSING THOUGHTS

Whew! We covered a lot of ground. I hope you found some decent takeaways in the first section of personal anecdotes. It was fun for me to recount some of my formative experiences. If it made you laugh just once at my expense, it will have been worth penning the stories!

Next, I wrote about the bread and butter of getting started working remotely: your environment. Whether it's your workspace, WiFi, or your wardrobe, the key is make sure you're as comfortable as possible and positioned for peak productivity.

Lastly, I covered the habits of a quality remote worker. At the end of the day, we're all human, and have different ways of managing, communicating, learning, and coping with being in different environments.

That said, there's no one-size-fits-all advice that anyone can dispense. We can all share our successes and trials, though, and learn from each other's experiences. I encourage you to reach out to other remote workers through artofworkingremotely.com, #remotechat, or any of the other fantastic networks that are *(or will be)* available to support this fantastic way of working.

Thank you so much for reading! I'd be eternally grateful if you'd pay it forward: gift a copy to a fellow remote worker who you think would appreciate it. If you enjoyed the book, I'd also be grateful for a review.

Remotely yours,

Scott

Scott Dawson